Why, God?

Burton Z. Cooper

John Knox Press
ATLANTA

Unless otherwise indicated Scripture quotations are from the Revised Standard Version of the Holy Bible, copyright, 1946, 1952 and © 1971, 1973 by the Division of Christian Education, National Council of the Churches of Christ in the U.S.A. and used by permission.

Acknowledgment is made to the following publishers:

Macmillan Publishing Co., for permission to quote from *The Brothers Karamazov* by Fyodor Doestoevsky, translated from the Russian by Constance Garnett (New York: Macmillan, 1923). Also for excerpt from *Letters and Papers from Prison,* Revised, Enlarged Edition, by Dietrich Bonhoeffer. Copyright © 1953, 1967, 1971 SCM Press Ltd.

Contemporary Books, Inc. for permission to quote from *Growing Up.* Reprinted from *Growing Up* © 1982 by Russell Baker, used with permission of Contemporary Books, Inc., Chicago.

The New York Review of Books for permission to quote from the 8-16-84 Joseph Brodsky article. Reprinted with permission from *The New York Review of Books.* Copyright © 1984 Nyrev, Inc.

Library of Congress Cataloging-in-Publication Data

Cooper, Burton Z., 1932–
  Why, God?

  1. Theodicy. I. Title.
BT160.C66 1988   231'.8   87-21499
ISBN 0-8042-0731-3

© copyright John Knox Press 1988
10 9 8 7 6 5 4 3 2 1
Printed in the United States of America
John Knox Press
Atlanta, Georgia 30365

Preface

"In the middle of my journey," Dante writes, "I came upon a dark wood." And so, too, did I. Dante had the good fortune to be able to speak about that inner darkness with the voice and mind of a great poet. I speak only with the voice and mind of a professional theologian.

Still, I have sought to find my own voice so that I could write as straightforwardly as possible about my own reflections on the problem of evil for Christian faith. When I began to write, it seemed like such a simple thing to find my own voice, to find the tone appropriate to myself and to the subject matter. I discovered how difficult that could be for a person professionally formed by a life of reading, interpreting, teaching, and writing upon the thoughts of others. Whether I have succeeded in that task, the reader must decide.

I did not write this book for the world of scholarship, though I hope that scholars will find some value in my arguments regarding this most difficult of faith's existential problems. Nor did I write this as a textbook for clergy and students, nor as a popular theology book for laypeople—although I hope that students, clergy, and especially laypeople will find much that is helpful here for the growth and strengthening of their faith.

This book is written for the church by a lay theologian who worships in and is committed to the church. It is written for those who are in the church but whose faith is troubled by a dissatisfaction with traditional resolutions to the problem of evil. It is also written for those who long ago (or short ago) had their faith driven out by their sensitivity to the world's suffering, or by the pain of their own suffering, but who nonetheless remain haunted by the sense of a divine reality in and behind things.

These friends did what they could to save my manuscript from awkward phrases and unclear thoughts: David Banks, Johanna Bos, Tom Dean, Craig Dykstra, David Hester, Helen Jones, Patricia Jean Manion, John Mulder, Lewis Shaw, Jenny Stone-Banks, Gunnar Urang, Louis Weeks.

Thanks also for the heavy involvement of my family: Blanche, Elizabeth, Stephen, Earl, and Hope, who suggested the title. And thanks to Louisville Presbyterian Seminary for sabbatical time and for financing the typing, and to Gay Alexander and Reba Cardwell for the typing.

Finally, I give thanks for my teacher Daniel Day Williams, dead now. I owe him much.

Contents

In memory of
SAMUEL PERCY COOPER
1967–1980

And the king was deeply moved, and went up to the chamber over the gate, and wept; and as he went, he said, "O my son Absalom, my son, my son Absalom! Would I had died instead of you, O Absalom, my son, my son!" (2 Samuel 18:33)

1

"Why, God?"
Waiting for an Answer

We are a sad company, those of us who seek to resolve the problem of evil. Somehow what we seek to explain eludes us. Some questions always remain unanswered, loose ends, conclusions that leave us uneasy, feelings of dissatisfaction. In some sense, this is true of all theological doctrines, but there is a difference when we talk about the problem of evil. Here we are talking about suffering: the suffering that others inflict on us and our loved ones, the suffering that comes to us by way of accident or disease or natural disaster, the suffering that, tragically, we inflict on others—sometimes knowingly, sometimes unknowingly.

The great Danish theologian, Søren Kierkegaard, used to inveigh against theologians who wrote about matters of faith and salvation as if they were objective commentators, and not, like the rest of us, suffering individuals caught in life's struggle. Some theological books seem disconnected from life's struggle. This is not one of them. I do not mean to suggest a direct correlation between pain and insight, as if the more we suffer, the more insight we gain. Intensity of feeling is not necessarily a barometer of truth. Often the opposite is the case. But those who allow their suffering to inform the way they think about the world can surely become more sensitive to the truth of the human situation. One of the sadder aspects of life is that painful experiences do not necessarily mature us—either morally or intellectually. Indeed, pain can lead us to become more selfish, more paranoid, more brutal. Still, our maturing does not take place apart from physical and mental pain.

In the film *Gandhi* there is a scene in which Gandhi confronts a Muslim who has killed a Hindu child in the religious riots that followed Indian independence. The man had deliberately killed because his own little boy had been murdered by Hindus. Here is an example, albeit an extreme one, of how suffering can brutalize us. Out of our own suffering, we inflict suffering on others, thereby adding our own energy to the spinning cycle of horror. Gandhi responded to this bereaved father—this child-murderer—by telling him to find a Hindu boy orphaned in the rioting to bring up as his own son.

We do not know whether this man took Gandhi's advice. Perhaps the combined weight of guilt and hatred was too much for him—guilt from murdering another's child, hatred for those who murdered his—so that he collapsed under the strain and became incapable of responsible action. Perhaps he had other children so that, in time, the intensity of his loss diminished and he was able to pick up his old life with its old loves and its old hatreds. Or perhaps he took Gandhi's advice, only to find it did not work because neither he nor the orphaned boy could overcome the bitterness of their past. Or perhaps it did work out and both he and the boy went on to . . . to what? to new life? to greater life? to redemptive life? Can we say that? Do we know what we are talking about?

This story comes out of the history and religion of a nation of which most of us have little knowledge. Yet we recognize in it the pathos of the human situation, because the problem of evil and suffering is a universal one. None of us is immune to the power of evil, either inflicted upon us from without or erupting from within. Is there something that poor Muslim father could have done that would have assured his son's life into adulthood? Was there anything in his life that could have given him any inkling that he could commit an evil as monstrous as the killing of a child?

Of course, there are ways in which we protect ourselves from the questions raised by such stories. We convince ourselves that these horrors happen to other people. We tell ourselves that we are neither Hindus nor Muslims, that we do not live in a country which gets caught up in religious riots, that we are more secure from the afflictions of evil than other people. This is understandable. If we are to have a life with the joys of family, friends, children, work, play, then we need some sense of security. We need to sense that we can count on what we have, and that the future will not undo us. Into our need for relative stability, order, and security, evil erupts with destructive force.

In destroying outer things, evil destroys inner things as well. The grief-stricken father whose child was killed by Hindus not only lost his son, he lost his inner moorings and his way of life. He suffered not only because the boy he loved and who loved him was no longer there to love and be loved but also because he had become something he had not been: a parent mad with bereavement, a rioting Muslim, a murderer of an innocent child, a guilt-ridden human being. The mystery of evil is not simply senseless destruction. It is senseless destruction that multiplies upon itself. It is a cancer for which the world serves as host.

We know there is evil in the world, and that innocent individuals suffer greatly. Groups of people, and sometimes whole societies, suffer well beyond what we might think their "just" deserts. We know that the evil which occasions our suffering takes many forms and has complex causes. Evil comes to us through the destructive powers of nature: through tornadoes and blizzards which tear through human communities taking lives and wreaking havoc; through disease which works from the inside, eating away at living tissue and destroying vital organs; through earthquakes which literally break the ground on which we stand. We think of these as natural evils, as forces which destroy, but not intentionally, because natural forces have no personal will.

There is also the evil which human beings inflict on each other. Its name is legion; we need simply look around, watch the evening news on television, read the daily newspaper, study history, or read the Bible, to find its particular name. Last night—it could have been any night in any place—on the eleven o'clock news, I heard the story of a family of four, three of whose members, the father, mother, and young boy, were bludgeoned to death. The fourth, a little girl, is in critical condition. The father had only recently been appointed editor of the local paper. The family, apparently, had much to anticipate. The news continued with reports of deaths in Lebanon where Christians, Muslims, and Druses have not yet learned to live peacefully amidst each other. In this respect, they are like Protestants and Catholics in Northern Ireland, the Israelis and Arabs in the Middle East, the Afrikaners and Blacks in South Africa. The list could go on. There are terrorist groups, police states, anti-Semitism, political repression, rape, kidnapping, and racist and sexist institutions and practices. In the shadow of all the evils we bring upon ourselves lies the possibility of nuclear warfare. Here, evil on earth approaches its total form, for nuclear warfare threatens all life on this planet.

A third, hybrid form of evil is perhaps the most common form. It does not arise out of our will to destroy but out of human negligence or ignorance or apathy toward the welfare of others or even ourselves. Children who suffer permanent brain damage by licking lead-filled paint on their cribs during infancy are the victims of neither an accident nor the intent of human will. The same is true of children with cancer-ridden bodies whose disease stems from having been raised in a community where the water supply has been contaminated by seepage from chemical dumps or the use of toxic sprays on nearby fruit orchards. Workers in asbestos plants in the 1940s and 1950s and their families who lived nearby did not know that the snow-like, particle-filled air they breathed would destroy their lungs. This list, also, could be endless. It includes those who are victims of careless driving, household accidents, medical malpractice, work-or play-related accidents, or harmful substances in our food and drugs. It includes those who suffer from negligence, ignorance, or apathy in our nursing homes, day-care centers, schools, or even in the home with our much-troubled marital and family life. Do incompetent, harried, or tired doctors, nurses, or teachers intend to harm their patients or students? Do marriages fail because parents intend to hurt their children or themselves?

Discussions of evil often come back to children—not because children are completely innocent or because adults always deserve the suffering they get. Neither seems to be the case. Rather, the suffering of children starkly exemplifies the combination of powerlessness and undeservedness which lies at the heart of the problem of evil. Even more than adults, young children lack the ability to protect themselves, and their severe suffering is out of all proportion to their faults or to any lesson they might possibly learn. The case of a suffering child, particularly where that suffering is senseless and ultimately fatal—whether due to forces of nature or human intent or insufficient attention—states the problem of evil in letters large enough for all to see. Or so it would seem.

There are those who argue that we neither know what evil is until we recognize it in ourselves nor know what suffering is until we endure it. I am reminded here of Martin Buber's insistence that a person "only knows factually what 'evil' is insofar as he knows about himself, everything else to which he gives this name is merely mirrored illusion." (Martin Buber, *Good and Evil*, [New York: Scribner's, 1952], p. 88.) Buber wants to call attention to the necessarily existential character of the knowledge of evil. I "know" evil when I acknowledge my own temptations and tendencies to be destructive. I "know" evil when I experience its presence within me. Similarly, I "know" the meaning of suffering only when evil has struck me or someone I love. There is, of course, truth in this existential perspective. None of us could bear to watch the evening news or read the morning paper if we knew the meaning of an assassination as the family of the assassinated person knows it, or if we knew the meaning of having our homes and villages flattened into rubble by bombing war-planes or washed away by flooding rains as do those whose stricken faces flicker momentarily across our TV screens.

It is often said of Western visitors to India that they are psychologically devastated by their first day in that country. They are taken aback by the sight of so many hungry and homeless people on the streets of the great cities. But this feeling is usually short-lived. Most Westerners soon find themselves able to walk the streets without any of the pain which the sight of so much human misery would normally cause them. They cease, so to speak, to "know" the misery. I do not cite this as an example of human evil but of the way we unconsciously protect ourselves from experiences which threaten our ability to affirm the goodness and feel the joys of our own life. Like Dante in the *Inferno*, we "look and pass" that which we find intensely painful.

There are exceptions to this generalization, though they may once again prove the rule. William James, the great American philosopher, tells us that as a young man he visited a mental institution where he saw a patient who spent his days crouched in a corner staring into space. James had been given much in life: an excellent education, high intelligence, a wealthy and caring family. Yet he fell into a lengthy state of despondency because he allowed himself to think that what happened to that person could happen to him, and if it did, he could do nothing about it. James felt, or knew from within, the destructive power of evil by experiencing it vicariously and refusing to say, "not me." But in opening himself to the evil that was working in the life of another he nearly suffered permanent damage to his own mental health.

For the most part we say, "not me," sometimes consciously, most times unconsciously. We "look and pass" because we instinctively sense that our will to live would be weakened even by the thought that the evil that strikes other people might also strike us or those we love. We love and live for our children, our spouses, our work, our causes, our nation, our way of life, our religious beliefs, ourselves. When something or someone that we live for is destroyed, a source of our will to live has been destroyed. We do not always know how much of our will to affirm life depends upon those people or things we love. C. S. Lewis, the British author who in 1940 wrote a widely read, intelligently argued book on Christian faith and evil, experienced in later life the apparent collapse of his faith under the blow of his beloved wife's death from cancer. For weeks after her death, Lewis was in despair. In a journal he kept at the time, Lewis described his faith as "a house of cards" and went on to write:

> If I had really cared, as I thought I did, about the sorrows of the world, I should not have been so overwhelmed when my own sorrow came. It

has been an imaginary faith playing with innocuous counters labelled "Illness", "Pain", "Death" and "Loneliness". I thought I trusted the rope until it mattered to me whether it would bear me. Now it matters, and I find I didn't. (C. S. Lewis, *A Grief Observed*, [New York: Seabury Press, 1961], p. 31.)

Lewis had assumed that his faith would sustain him through the worst onslaught of evil. What he discovered was that only a direct experience of real loss tested the reality of his ability to withstand the withering powers of evil. In hindsight, Lewis called his faith imaginary; he could just as well, and perhaps more accurately, have called his earlier understanding of evil imaginary. In 1940, when he wrote *The Problem of Pain*, Lewis thought he had taken the measure of faith and evil. In 1960, in late middle age, reeling with despair, he knew that evil was more powerful than he had imagined. Now that he knew what evil was "factually," to use Buber's term, and not simply imaginatively, he found himself again raising questions that he thought he had answered twenty years earlier. Only this time the questions had a different force because the problem was in his own life. It had become "existential."

In *The Problem of Pain*, Lewis wrote that his task was "only to discover how, perceiving a suffering world, and being assured on quite different grounds, that God is good, we are to conceive that goodness and that suffering without contradiction." (C. S. Lewis, *The Problem of Pain*, [New York: Macmillan, 1944], p. 24.) What he sought to resolve in 1940 was the intellectual problem raised for Christian faith by the logical contradiction between the perception of worldly suffering and the knowledge of divine goodness. It is interesting that in his preface Lewis specifically disavowed the task of teaching people how their faith might help them bear pain. (Lewis, *Pain*, pp. vii–viii.)

Lewis's honesty about what he was and was not doing indirectly raises a helpful question for us in our struggles with the problem of evil. Does it matter what we make our starting point for understanding and dealing with the destructive power of evil in our lives? Perhaps Lewis's very way of beginning misleads him. It is a startling fact that key biblical texts on suffering and evil begin not with the perception of a suffering world but with a suffering people.

The book of Exodus begins with God "hearing" the suffering of an enslaved people; the book of Job is a dialogue between a suffering person and his "consoling" friends; the gospels and epistles of the early church emerge from a persecuted community who confess a crucified Lord. These texts suggest that the way into understanding the relation of biblical faith to evil is through the suffering of oneself or one's people. Perhaps Lewis's earlier separation of pain as an intellectual problem from pain as an immediate experience accounts for his rather unhelpful insistence that Christianity

> creates, rather than solves, the problem of pain, *for pain would be no problem* [my emphasis] unless, side by side with our daily experiences of this painful world, we had received what we think a good assurance that ultimate reality is righteous and loving. (Lewis, *Pain,* p. 12.)

This kind of argument, unfortunately, obscures the real situation of Christian faith. It is true, of course, that the experience of evil threatens our belief in God. But we will not achieve the proper formulation of the problem of evil for Christian faith unless we see that it is also true that the reality of faith stands against and overcomes the power of evil. It is this reality that is the "assurance" of Christian faith.

Christianity is characterized by believers who participate in a community of faith which experiences God's power over evil in their own lives. Lewis's later book, *A Grief Observed,* records his despairing response to his wife's death. Yet that record of pain implicitly witnesses to hope. In the depth of his despair Lewis never ceased to struggle toward a level of faith which could heal the destructive bitterness of soul that had taken hold of him. He assumed, apparently apart from any consciously formulated belief, that even a "collapsed" faith points the believer toward the participation in a redemptive power which can conquer the destructive forces of evil.

Lewis's two books on evil are separated by twenty years. More significantly, they are separated by a searing experience of personal loss. Together they reflect the tension caused by the two-handedness of the life of faith. On one hand, we perceive evil in the world and we seek to understand it in the light of our belief in a loving God. On the other hand, we are suffering individuals who seek redemption from dark forces that threaten to overcome us. Books may separate these two aspects of faith, sometimes in a helpful way, other times in a way that misleads us. In life, of course, they come together. We do not have our faith simply in terms of right confessional statements or strong theological arguments. Nor do we have our faith simply by living out certain inarticulated or pre-reflective truths. Christianity does not stand so much between these extremes as it is formed and informed by each of them.

But how can we reflect upon our faith in a way that helps us deal with our own suffering and with the suffering of others?

Some years ago, caught up in my own grief, I went frantically to those books which talked about the meaning of death and suffering. I found no solace. Perhaps I was inwardly shouting questions which books do not answer: Why did this have to happen to me? Where is the comfort of God now? How can I, my wife, my living children, live with this pain? It is my sorrow to be able to speak out of my own experience. In 1965, my daughter Jennifer, just two months shy of her fifth birthday, died quite unexpectedly from a bacteriological infection in her lungs. Then, incredibly, in January 1980, my twelve-year-old son, Samuel, died of cardiac arrest, apparently caused by no more than one of his typical asthma attacks.

I was a graduate student at Union Seminary at the time of Jennifer's death. I told a friend, a fellow graduate student, that I was waiting for him or anyone else in this religious, academic community to help me deal theologically with this. He answered, "We are waiting for you to help us." At the time, it struck me as an ironic remark. I, who was suffering from the death of a beloved child, was supposed to help him whose children lived. But of course, I had misunderstood him. He meant that he felt theologically helpless before me because he did not know how theology could meet the concrete needs of a particular suffering person. And I did not know either—not even where to begin. I knew only anguish. The God who comforted and strengthened seemed very far away, and all theological talk seemed irrelevant.

What I needed was both the comfort of God *and* a relevant theology. Those two needs came together in my mind as if I could not have one without the other. I am, as Kierkegaard was wont to say, a poor, suffering, existing individual, but I am also a theologian. What strength my faith can have depends on my bringing these two together. To a certain extent, this is true of all Christians. We are in a tradition which gives weight to words: scriptural words, creedal words, words of worship, words of counsel, preached words, dogmatic words, denominational words.

Some years ago at a worship service a preacher leaned into the eerie silence that sometimes precedes a sermon and shouted, "Why, God?" The words had their desired effect: the preacher caught the attention of his congregation. But not simply because he startled them with a loud cry, but because these words, "Why, God?" echoed their own past cries. Hearing them stirred up their unhappy memories of pain and suffering. It reminded them of their theological uneasiness with the fact that terrible things happen in a world which they confess to be created by a loving, all-powerful deity. Lewis's insistence that Christianity creates the problem of evil may not be quite on target, but it is true that Christian faith allows us no rest in our struggle to understand and withstand the power of evil. Because of this, there can never be anything neat about Christian attempts to resolve the problem of evil, if by "neat" we mean a justification of it. Too often, the attempt to justify God ends up justifying evil. Those arguments which succeed too well in justifying the presence of evil in the world actually do a disservice to the Christian faith.

There is another reason why Christian theology should avoid neatness when it addresses the problem of evil. The resolution of that problem necessarily involves us in thinking things through for ourselves. Reflection upon the meaning of evil is not like drawing the necessary conclusion to a logical line of argument. It is more like making a judgment from insufficient and ambiguous evidence. Whitehead's remark that "religion is what a person does with his solitariness" underscores this point. Whitehead knows well that our knowledge of God and growth in the religious life depend partly on others. But the assent to God always has to be *our* assent. Whatever else others can do for me, they cannot believe for me. Whatever else logical analysis can do for me, it cannot make my decisions of faith. When I am hurting all over from the loss of someone I love or from the sight of terrible suffering, theological analysis cannot tell me whether I shall continue to believe in God.

In times of suffering, we are sometimes told to "hold the faith." The meaning of this phrase is not entirely clear. It looks like a command, as if the speaker is using his or her authority to bolster our threatened faith. It could also express solicitude. The speaker is letting us know that he or she cares enough about us to want us to continue in our faith. Or the phrase could be expressing the speaker's recognition that we are suffering deeply, even to the point of loss of faith. But there is one other meaning implicit in this phrase which is germane to the discussion. When we are told to "hold the faith," the speaker is reminding us that though we have been buffeted about cruelly by events, it is not the events or even our suffering that determines our decision. It is the self in the mystery of its freedom or, as Whitehead says, in its solitariness, which determines our decision.

An example, which is more than an example, of the inner dynamic to which I refer can be found in one of the great passages of world literature: the conversation on faith and suffering between two brothers, Ivan and Alyosha, in Dostoevsky's *The Brothers Karamazov*. Ivan has long pondered the amount and forms of evil and suffering in the world. He recites to Alyosha a frightful litany of human meanness, cruelty, and suffering. Ivan argues that nothing can justify so much pain, not even an ultimate harmony. A single death by torture of a young, trusting child is compensated for neither by a later judgment nor a later harmony. Ivan is not arguing atheism; his intent is not to deny but to indict God. It is God's love, not God's existence, that he holds under question. Love, Ivan believes, whether ours or God's, would find the extreme forms of pain in this world too high a price to pay for even the highest end. The indictment of God carries with it the indictment of life. "It is not God that I don't accept," Ivan says, "only I most respectfully return him the ticket." Because there is suffering in the world, Ivan argues, life is intolerable for a caring, sensitive person.

Alyosha listens intently to Ivan. He sympathizes with almost everything he says except the indictment of God which he calls "rebellion." Still, he agrees that he would not consent to a single child's death by torture, even for an ultimate harmony. At the end of the discussion, Alyosha kisses Ivan.

Ivan and Alyosha see the same world. Innocent people, even children, sometimes suffer horribly; and cruel people often prosper, sometimes outrageously. They agree that there can be no justification for these extremities of suffering and moral injustice. Where they differ is in their response to the presence of evil and suffering in the world. Ivan responds by condemning God and finding life not worth the price of its existence. Alyosha responds by looking to Christ and going out to the suffering other in compassion. Their unblinking look at evil and suffering, then, does not determine their particular responses, but it does bring both of them to an ultimate decision about God, Christ, and the character of their life. By facing the world as it really is, by not trying to justify the evil in it, by refusing to say "not me," they bring themselves to that inner place where their decision affects the very depths of their personhood. In Alyosha's case, his decision moves him toward fulfillment; in Ivan's, it leads him toward despair.

Of course, literature can overdramatize. Most of us do not make decisions, as did Alyosha and Ivan, that move us so starkly to contrasting poles. But some of the decisions we make are ultimate decisions, particularly those which are in response to extreme suffering. Others may be many, seemingly insignificant ones, which move us only little by little. Still, these small decisions participate in ultimacy if they are moving us either to bitterness of being and loss of faith or to increased sensitivity to the suffering of others and a deepening of faith. These are free decisions though not in any absolute sense; even free decisions are partly shaped by our past life and our present conditions.

Our decisions emerge from our ability to shape our personhood out of all those forces, inner and outer ones, past and present ones, which affect our being. We are free not because past events do not affect our being—surely that would be a false definition of freedom—but because there is an element of self-determination in our decision making. In the final analysis, it is not our past that makes us but we who make ourselves out of our past.

I am charting a position here somewhat against both those who argue that our ultimate decisions emerge strictly from our sociological and psychological background and those who argue that God's grace irresistibly shapes those decisions. The former have been too much influenced by the methodological model of the physical sciences, which understands the behavior of physical entities entirely in terms of preceding causes. The latter, oddly enough, have been too much influenced by the model of the absolute king who has the power to enforce his will on his subjects. We need to understand God's power and love in a way which reflects God's respecting and working with our freedom rather than manipulating or overriding it.

If we take the position that there is a moment of freedom or solitariness in the decision-making process of the self, then we can make some sense of why theological analysis seems relevant to us in our understanding of evil and suffering, and yet, in times of crisis, seems not relevant at all. In a time of extreme suffering, when we are dealing with death or loss and are plagued with a sense of emptiness or guilt or meaninglessness, we find ourselves facing ultimate powers and being asked to make ultimate decisions.

The terrible events that are causing our suffering bear a heavy weight in our decision making, but they do not bear the only weight. Past events in our lives and our reactions to them, the kinds of communities to which we belong, our past beliefs, values, and understandings are all germane to how we respond now. And yet, for all that, we are literally and spiritually alone in the moment of decision. We are separated from others because it is our agony and only indirectly theirs, and therefore, the decision can only be ours. We are separated from our past decisions and understandings precisely because something has happened which calls into question the grounds on which we made those decisions. When we say, or feel, in our suffering that our understanding or theology seems irrelevant, we mean one of two things. We mean that we have discovered the limits of analysis, that analysis in itself cannot make our ultimate decisions. Or we mean that our past analysis is inadequate, that we have just experienced something which makes no sense in terms of our theological understanding. Of course, in most cases we probably mean both.

The cry "Why, God?" suggests that even in our anguish, when our past understanding does not help us, we have not so much given up on understanding as we are crying out for a new, more inclusive one. There is no single or simple meaning to those anguished words. They sometimes mean, "Why are you doing this to me, God?" Those who mean this perhaps believe that all events, both joyous and painful ones, come from God's will and that we are to accept our suffering in faith and, if possible, discover God's good intention hidden in them. Or they sometimes function not so much as a question but as an indictment, a verbal shaking of our fist at God, who either willed this horror or could have prevented it. Or these words could reflect a certain naïveté about the nature and reality of evil. Do we not sometimes hear people say, "I did not think that such a terrible thing could occur"? Or, perhaps most profoundly, these words can mean, "Why, God, am I experiencing you as an enemy (or as a void) when I have known you as a friend, redeemer, companion, comforter?" When this is what we mean, we are presupposing the belief in God's healing power. What we cannot understand is its absence in a time when we sorely need it.

This analysis is not exhaustive. But whatever meaning lies behind the words "Why, God?" the fact that we cry them indicates that we are desperately looking for further answers. Even after we have made the move of faith, there are always unresolved questions that must be dealt with. "Dealing with" may sometimes mean no more than continuing to seek understanding. In *The Brothers Karamazov,* Alyosha's response to those who inflict evil on others and those who suffer from evil reflects a profoundly understood and embodied faith, a faith which is certainly "whole." But wholeness of faith does not preclude the presence of unresolved questions of faith. Alyosha, no more than Ivan, can understand how God's love can live side by side with a child's senseless, cruel death by torture.

It is true, then, that a profound feeling for and understanding of God's love and forgiveness through Jesus Christ can be enough for a fullness of faith. But it is also true that events can shake our faith as Lewis's was shaken and, perhaps, as Ivan's was shaken. Theological reflection is neither our only help nor our most important help. But it can help us deal with troubling questions which sometimes grasp us and which, if left unheeded, weaken our faith. Theological help neither means that our pain will cease nor that we will forget our suffering. But it may broaden or alter our understanding of God, Christ, and church in such a way that we open ourselves more effectively to God's redemptive power. The chapters that follow reflect, in part, my own personal and professional odyssey. There were questions that I asked years ago out of my own pain, though even when I first asked them I knew they were age-old questions: Where is God the comforter? How can I bear this suffering? How will I ever affirm life again? The answers, I discovered, come very slowly. They have to wait upon life and thought. That seems obvious enough now; it did not seem so then.

This book, insofar as words will allow, represents those answers. They fall under three large headings: God is vulnerable; God's redemptive power is suffering love known to us especially in Jesus Christ; the church is the new community embodying in its fallible, ambiguous way the transforming, healing power of Christ in the world. The exposition of these headings is biblical and experiential. In many places, perhaps even at its heart, it is not traditional. The theological tradition has tended to downplay and sometimes "lose" those biblical texts which suggest not divine control of history but God's risk in history. These "lost" texts affirm not an absolute, immutable God but a vulnerable, dynamic God who suffers from our faithless responses and suffers with our suffering. The result of ignoring these texts has been to obscure and hamper Christian reflection on evil and suffering. On the other hand, the understanding of God as vulnerable helps clarify the relation of God to evil in a way that removes certain barriers to our faith and, more significantly, frees us to define God through the power manifest in the cross of Christ.

This shift in our understanding from an invulnerable to a vulnerable God leads to a shift in where we look for Christian faith's answer to evil. We have tended to focus primarily on the mystery of God's controlling will and power, both to account for the presence of evil and to comfort ourselves about its ultimate defeat. This book asks us to shift our focus to the cross of Christ for the clue to the character of God's power over evil and to the church as that new community holding up and seeking to embody that power in its life. When we look for the answer to evil in a different place, we come to change our understanding of the answer. Why we should shift our focus and how we can re-understand the answer of Christian faith to evil is what this book is about.

2

On the Outer Edge
of the Tradition

"What we feel is that God has answered our prayers."

The words are those of the mother of an eighteen-year-old marine stationed in Lebanon. She had just been informed that her son survived the Sunday morning terrorist bomb attack on a U.S. Marines barracks in Beirut. The family had lived in fear for over twenty-four hours that their son was among the 241 dead.

I saw this woman's joyous face on the Monday evening news and though my heart went out to her, I worried about those families who would not receive happy news. How would they hear her words? That news was very slow in coming; identification of the dead was difficult because the ton of dynamite that blasted the building destroyed all the personnel records. By late Tuesday, official word began to come through; next of kin were being personally notified in their homes by members of the Marine Corps. Again, the television cameras were there; this time, mercifully and intelligently barred from the house, they were waiting outside in the garden. As we watched the television screen, the cameras picked out, in the night's darkness, three marines in full dress uniform. Messengers of death, they walked up the path, knocked on the door and, then, from the darkened television screen came the cries of anguish and the scream, "Oh God, no!"

These two stories tell us of two families agonizingly caught in a life and death drama. They also depict for us, when we are finally able to get some emotional distance from them, the joyous beliefs and the anguished faith of people spontaneously expressing God's presence in heartfelt events of their life. In doing so, these stories dramatize the theological difficulties that continue to bedevil Christianity's attempts to reconcile faith in a loving, all-powerful God with the evil and suffering encountered in actual life.

We do not know, of course, whether the woman who said, "God answered our prayers," would go on to say that for good reasons, perhaps known only to God, the prayers of the wives and parents of the dead marines were left unanswered. Nor do we know whether that other cry, "Oh God, no," expressed not only terrible anguish, but the belief, which lingers grammatically in the words, that nothing happens outside God's will. We do not know these people's innermost convictions, nor do we know the faith struggles precipitated in their lives by the sudden, violent death of loved ones who must have seemed to them innocent, decent, and promising young people.

What we do know and can study is the theological tradition which shapes our faith and which, in good part, lies behind our ideas about God and the way we interpret pain and suffering in our lives. We tend to think that our ideas about God are simply biblical, but the word biblical can cover a multitude of conflicting interpretations—as the sad history of interpersonal and interdenominational contentiousness in the church suggests. The way we interpret the Bible and the particular texts we emphasize have as much to do with the theological tradition as with the Bible itself. The theological tradition has lifted out and stressed those biblical texts which suggest God's control of events and ignored or interpreted away those which suggest otherwise. This way of reading the Bible and understanding Christian faith has radically affected our approach to the problem of evil. We too often fail to recognize that Scripture's attitude toward the notion of divine control is considerably more ambiguous than that of the tradition. But that issue I leave for the following chapter.

We must first discuss the theological tradition. We need to do this not as an academic exercise that one must go through before saying something new, but to understand the reasons for its power and authority over us. We must discover what is at stake in the traditional notion of God. Why is it that despite the injustices and moral incongruities that we daily witness or read about, we continue to hold to the notion of God as all-controlling, all-powerful, all-knowing, invulnerable and unchanging? Further, we need to look at those places where the tradition itself questions its own understanding of God's nature and power.

I do not mean to suggest that the tradition is monolithic or unchanging, as if what we find in Augustine is identical to what we find in Calvin. The term *tradition* refers to the ongoing development of a mainstream of theological thought which has both formed and, in its turn, been formed by creative theologians in the church, particularly by Augustine, Aquinas, Luther, Calvin, Wesley, and Barth. Within the tradition there have been a variety of answers to the problem of evil, though the variety has been more a matter of shifting emphases than disagreement about matters of substance. Aquinas, for example, and those who follow him tend to seek a rational justification for pain and suffering, while Luther sees our inability to justify evil as a sign that faith alone is the ground of belief in a living God. Yet Aquinas, like Luther, knows that reason has limits, and it was Aquinas who was so deeply moved by an intense religious vision that he likened his own system to "chaff."

Thus there are unifying elements among a particular group of creative theologians which allow us to talk about an ongoing theological tradition. Of particular importance to the problem of evil is the common assumption in the tradition of the absolute or controlling character of God's power. Consider the way the tradition understands the meaning of God's will and knowledge. Aquinas writes, "Not only that things are done which God wills to be done, but also that they are done in the way that He wills." (Thomas Aquinas, *Summa Theologica*, [in *Introduction to St. Thomas Aquinas*, ed. A. C. Pegis; New York: Modern Library, 1948], Ia.19.8.) Calvin says that God "foresees future events only by reason of the fact that he decreed that they take place." (John Calvin, *Institutes of the Christian Religion,* [Library of Christian Classics, 21; Philadelphia: Westminster, 1960], III.23.6.) It is not that things happen and then God knows them, which is the way it is for us. Rather, it is because God knows things or decrees them that they happen. The tradition interprets God's knowledge and will in such a way that knowledge, will, and power come to one and the same thing. Or consider the notion of eternity which Augustine established as the defining characteristic of God. Our way of being is sequential; one event follows another like the frames in a movie. God's way of being is simultaneous; all events are present at once, as if all the frames of a film were seen at the same time on some huge screen. Eternity, also, means power. What is simultaneously present in God's will or decrees or knowledge must, in time, be worked out in the creation. The notion of predestination, which Calvin stressed, flows directly from this Augustinian interpretation of eternity. In fact, Augustine, Aquinas, and Luther, in different ways, suggest a predestinarian view of God.

Consider now the notion of divine independence as also expressing the absolute character of God's power. Emil Brunner, the German contemporary of Barth, once devised the following formulas: God minus the world equals God; the world minus God equals zero. Brunner thus expresses the belief that the world does not have sufficient power to exist without God but God could exist without the world. The formulas serve to contrast the creator and the creation. *We* need relationships with others to exist: parents to give us birth, feed us, and love us; others to help us gain a sense of identity and give us purpose in life. God, however, needs no relationships with others to be God. But does Brunner also mean to suggest that God minus the world, God without relationships, is the same as God with the world? This question raises some difficult issues about the meaning of God's perfection and sovereignty.

The tradition has held that God is the same from eternity. This affirmation of God's immutability is rooted in the assumption that the divine reality is complete in itself. "Completion" is understood as the perfect form of power. If we say that God is complete, that God is what God is quite apart from anything that we

Human freedom
Divine Sovereignty

might be or do, then we are saying that only God controls God. This is the power of invulnerability; it constitutes one side of the notion of independence. The other side concerns God's relation to our activities. Karl Barth, in maintaining the traditional interpretation of God's sovereignty, argues that God's activities are in and behind our activities—that, for example, it is God who does what Moses and David do, what the earth, the sun, and the rain do. (Karl Barth, *Church Dogmatics,* [Edinburgh: T. & T. Clark, 1960], III, 3, pp. 132–33.) In language reminiscent of Aquinas's doctrine that God is the primary cause of our secondary causes, Barth writes, "the fact that He [God] controls it [our activities] means that He is the Lord of the creature even while it has its own activity. He controls its independent activity as such." (Barth, *Dogmatics,* III, 3, p. 165.)

Of course, Barth, as Aquinas before him, wants to affirm human freedom. But theologians within the tradition find it difficult to work out a coherent doctrine of human freedom because freedom raises what we can call the religious dilemma. When I affirm my freedom, I take responsibility for my decisions and actions. I feel responsible, in part, for the consequences of my actions upon the world; the world is different because I have lived. What I gain from this affirmation of freedom is a sense of personal meaningfulness: I matter. On the other hand, when I affirm my freedom I am also affirming the freedom of others. I then come to know the world as issuing from millions of individually made free decisions. But this understanding arouses in me fears of disorder and disconnectedness. History seems to lose its moorings and its goal. The consequence of this perspective is that my sense of belonging to this world and of feeling secure in it becomes threatened. Here, then, is the religious dilemma. The more I stress human freedom, the more I lay the ground for personal insecurity and historical meaninglessness. The more I stress divine sovereignty and control, the more I lay the ground for inner peace and historical meaning.

We are talking here about one of the unresolved tensions in our understanding of the meaning of faith. While there have always been voices in the church stressing human freedom—the Pelagians against Augustine, Erasmus against Luther, the Arminians against the Calvinists—the theologians who have formed the tradition have been more concerned to stress God's sovereign power and control. Perhaps they do this because they sense that the power of a redemptive faith lies not so much in the affirmation of human freedom as in the concrete assurance of salvation with its promise of peace. Luther, in particular, was dominated by the need to still the insecurities of the anxious heart and to bring the peace of God to the life of faith. And Calvin, for related reasons, stressed a divine plan, highlighted the doctrines of predestination and providence, and repeatedly quoted Psalm 115: "God does whatever he pleases." Calvin and Luther saw human freedom as sin and rebellion unless it is rooted in the security that comes from faith in God's sovereignty. Christian freedom, for the Reformers, primarily means freedom from the anxiety of works-righteousness or from the anxiety about the unknowability of the future. It is faith that frees us from anxiety, because faith provides the assurance that no matter what happens God is working in all things for our own good. Faith alone can make us both free and obedient servants of God.

This is a powerful understanding of freedom, but it is not a complete understanding. What is missing is the dimension of the indeterminateness, or openness, of personal and social history, the sense that our decisions really affect the way things go, and the affirmation that when we choose, we choose among genuine alternatives.

In their time, perhaps Luther and Calvin took the notion of freedom as far as they were able. Still, we live in other times. Our consciousness is gripped by the sense of the indeterminacy of our future and by the conviction that we do not have our humanity apart from our freedom to shape that future. We need to rethink the ways in which faith provides us with security in the light of our understanding of the openness of history. Even Barth, who holds that the operation of God's sovereignty is as predestinating as Calvinist teaching describes it (Barth, *Dogmatics*, III, 3, p. 131), also feels the need to affirm human freedom in its fullest sense. Barth knows that predestination and freedom contradict each other, but he argues, at least for the moment, that the problem is one of logic, not faith. In logic, he admits, there is a contradiction, but in faith we experience the compatibility of the two notions. (Barth, *Dogmatics,* III, 3, pp. 147, 182–84.)

If only that were the case. When things are going well we might convince ourselves that we experience both God's control over events in our life and our free decision-making process. But when we do, does not the issue return in a new form, and this time with more urgency, as soon as we experience some horrifying evil in our life or in the life of our people?

Consider, for example, the event in our own century that has become a symbol of evil: the Nazi extermination of six million Jews. When we think of the death camps, their gas chambers, their starving inmates, the children and babies torn from their mothers' arms, killed and buried in mass graves, can we say that, in faith, we experience the compatibility of divine sovereignty and human freedom? Even if we modify the tradition by arguing that in establishing an order for nature and in granting us freedom God places limits on divine power, does this "common sense" resolution not get dashed on the rocks of excessive evil? Although we so desperately want the self-limiting resolution to work, it always seems to work better in theory than in life because the notion of self-limits still contains within it the assumption that if God so chooses, God can unilaterally prevent any event from occurring. But how, then, can we help wondering why bullets find their fatal way into the bodies of John Kennedy, Bobby Kennedy, and Martin Luther King, Jr., while every assassination attempt on Adolf Hitler's life failed? Great evils appall us not only because they offend us morally but because they offend us religiously. We ask ourselves, "Where is God?" or "How can God bear this to happen?" We think that a loving God would have devised some way to limit such wantonly destructive actions without infringing on our sense of freedom or of natural probability. Or we cannot help feeling that surely the all-knowing God who commanded the world into existence could have created a world where the possibilities for evil and the extremities of pain were neither as many nor as intense as in this one.

We can see now what C. S. Lewis meant when he wrote that Christianity "creates rather than solves the problem of pain." Lewis did not mean that Christianity creates the problem of pain in existence. Pain is simply a fact of life and recognized in all religions. What Lewis had in mind was a very specific sort of theological problem. That problem has been traditionally formulated this way: if God does or can control all events, if nothing determines a divine action other than God's free will, if God is also known to us as all-wise, just and loving, then why do evil, injustice, and suffering cut so deeply and destructively into our lives?

There has been neither a shortage of answers to this question nor a shortage of questions to the answers. Perhaps the oldest, deepest rooted answer is that evil and suffering are the consequence of sin. The reason for the ancient, almost universal, character of this answer is not hard to understand. All human groups have a sense of right and wrong; indeed no human group could maintain itself for long without that sense. Negative consequences to our sinful actions demonstrate that it matters whether we do good or evil. When we believe that God punishes us for our sins through natural disasters, through disease and accidents, through the unjust social structures we create, or even through people who are all too willing to do evil to others, we are affirming a just God who insists that the world be moral.

When we ask whether there are not some innocent people who suffer, the tradition argues that no one is innocent. All of us have excessive concern for ourselves and those whom we love, and insufficient concern for others, particularly those whom we think of as strangers and enemies.

Of course, we cannot help noticing that there are some people, even religious people, who suffer well beyond their just deserts. The tradition seeks to help us here by suggesting that sometimes it is necessary to test a person's faith through inflicting some evil on them. Often our faith is not as strong as we thought it was and we need a time of trial to tell us that. Or it may be that if life is too agreeable to us that we will forget that eternal happiness can lie only with God and not in worldly goods which must inevitably pass from our grasp. God troubles us in order to warn us that there is a grave insufficiency in the way we are living our life. In any event, the tradition points out that we need to experience hardship and suffering, both our own and others', if we are to have any depth of character. How can we develop compassion unless we experience the suffering of others? How can we be drawn to sacrifice unless there is hardship in our midst?

If we ask why God could not have made us compassionate and just, and created us with depth of character, the tradition answers that God wants to create the best possible world. A world where we freely choose to love others and worship God is a better world than one where we do so out of necessity of nature.

The phrase "best possible world" is a strange, even upsetting, way of describing our world. For it is hard not to ask how this can be the best possible world when every day we see evil people prospering, and where poverty, crime, terrorism, war, and the threat of war seem to be increasing and not decreasing.

One of the ways that the tradition has dealt with this kind of question is by distinguishing between real evil and apparent evil. Sometimes a terrible thing happens to us in order to make possible some great good which otherwise would not have occurred. There are hidden meanings in those events which appear to be completely without meaning. Even such a great evil as the Nazi extermination of European Jews can be understood as making possible the rise of the state of Israel, a homeland for the biblical people who had been without their home for almost two thousand years.

This rejoinder of the tradition pits a great evil against the realization of a great hope. But when we think of the horror of the Holocaust can we say that there is any "good" which can justify it? Also, this particular "good" has its ironic dimension. The return of the Jews to their homeland deprived the Palestinians of theirs, and led to the establishment of Palestinian refugee camps and constant political turmoil, warfare, and terrorism in the Middle East.

The tradition, here, returns to its argument that sin is universal and that this is a "fallen" world. The Israelis, too, are sinners; they think more of resolving their own problems than the problems they are creating for others. Because we are sinful, because we can be tempted to demonic, destructive activities, we constantly sow the seeds of new evils in this world. We can never have any assurance, no matter what personal and social good we realize, that some unanticipated evil will not arise and befall us, our loved ones, and our world. Our ultimate consolation can never be in some worldly achievement but in eternal life. There is no other consolation with any force; either we believe in it or not.

The difficulty here is the one that troubled Dostoevsky, and which he portrayed dramatically through the tortured mind and questions of Ivan. Ivan asks, for all of us, how does the use of God's power to give us eternal life help us to understand how God can allow useless but horrible pain, pain which can be shut off only with death: the pain of the tortured or fatally diseased or monstrously deformed child or even the pain of the wounded, dying animal whose cries rend the forest?

The tradition gives one last answer. There are some things we can never understand. Only in faith can we believe that God is justified. We must continue to have faith that there is some good fruit, some meaning, some moral basis even for the unbearable sufferings of the innocent and helpless.

Does this last answer stop our questions? And if we do not stop questioning does that mean we have insufficient faith? When asked, "What was God doing before creating the world?" Luther responded that God was preparing hell for those who would ask that question. He meant that some questions are idle because they have no answer. If we let them work on us, they can only have destructive consequences to our faith. Often we feel that way about the problem of evil. We say to ourselves that if we do not stop thinking about it we will lose our faith. But there are times when we cannot stop thinking about it. Does the fault lie in us? in our faith? in our ideology?

The answer, surely, is not that the traditional justifications lack profundity. Much of the evil in this world is indeed inherited from our sinful past. Our tragically destructive Civil War reaped the whirlwind of our persistent maintenance of the institution of slavery. Calvin used to talk about God's "secret will," God's hidden way of bringing wrathful, righteous judgment upon an unrighteous world. Calvin's concept allows us to understand the Civil War as God's judgment upon slavery. Even the self-destructive fighting in Lebanon can be understood as issuing from God's secret will, God's judgment upon hostile factions who have difficulty seeking reconciliation with each other now because there was so much hatred in their past. And, surely, it is also true that deep suffering, even the willingness to endure suffering when it appears senseless, and sometimes even our willingness to love those who inflict suffering on us, can give us a wisdom and create a depth of soul that surprises our expectations. There is a wisdom of mind and a beauty of soul that seems to come only through the experience of tragedy. The problem is not that the tradition lacks profound insights into the nature of human suffering and evil; the problem is that the sum of the insights does not answer the problem of evil.

The situation of the tradition is much like that of a large family who for generations have lived in a big, old, drafty house with forty windows and thirty storm windows stored in the attic. In normal weather the family is comfortable in the house, but when the temperature drops below zero and the winds are fierce, cold air blows through the loosely-fitted windows chilling the house. The family runs to the attic for the storm windows and installs them on thirty of the windows, but because cold air is coming through the remaining ten, the house is still cold. Some members of the family rush about moving the storm windows from window to window, hoping to get a combination that will keep the house at least minimally warm. Others simply huddle around each other trying to generate a little warmth with their own body heat. A few leave the house. Finally the cold spell breaks, normal weather returns and the storm windows are taken back to the attic. Some members of the family think that it is unlikely that they will see weather like that again in their lifetime; others are not so sure. After a while they stop talking about it.

The family, of course, is us, the community of believers. The big, old, drafty house is the theological tradition. The storm windows are the varied ways the tradition seeks to justify God in the face of evil. Most of the time, it is enough that we know that there are some explanations stored in the attic, that is, in books or in the minds of theologians and clergy whom we consult in times of crisis. But when the cold winds of evil blow on us, we have difficulty with the answers. There never seem to be quite enough of them: there is always something left unanswered, so we keep on running around asking, "Why, God?" Finally, though a few people lose their faith and leave the house, most of us calm down. After all, it is a beautiful old house and it does offer more protection than any other house we know of. Also, the people we love live in it and their love did help us bear the cold. (The storm window image in this parable reaches back to William Hamilton's statement that "theology is always like having six storm windows to cover eight windows." *The New Essence of Christianity,* [New York: Association Press, 1966], p. 43.)

Perhaps the question we need to ask when the cold winds cease blowing on us is not, "Why, God?" but why do we never have enough answers, enough storm windows in the attic? We can get a clue into this by returning to the analysis of Calvin's "secret will." The notion seems to work well as long as we stay on the large scale. For example, the violence in Northern Ireland in the twentieth century is directly related to the earlier history of British violence and colonialism in Ireland. The flagrant violation by the British of God's love commandment in the past can be understood as finally reaping its negative consequences: the Protestants of Scottish descent live in fear; and the British economy, when it can least afford it, siphons off a good part of its budget to enforce the peace in Northern Ireland.

Of course we ask about the native Irish Catholic population. Do they not, also, live in fear? Are they not also being terrorized?

The answer is yes, but it could be argued that they are being punished for resorting to violence instead of seeking more peaceful, creative means toward a just reconciliation.

The problem comes when we move from the large scale to the particular scale, from the general to the specific. Because God's will is a particular will and not simply a general will, the tradition must say not simply that God wills the punishment of the British. It must also say that God wills the punishment in particular ways: these specific people explode these bombs in this place and these specific people die in that explosion, etc. Christian faith has to account not only for general punishment and suffering but also for the particularity or specificity of punishment and suffering. An Irish Christian mother is not being sentimental when she asks why God specifically willed that bomb to blow off her child's legs, nor is an English wife when she asks why God willed that her soldier-husband be killed by that sniper's bullet. When a six-year-old boy who has loving parents and is endowed with gifts of personality and intelligence is kidnapped, tortured, and murdered by some deranged person, the notion that such things can happen because we have flouted God's general command to create a just society does not explain why God specifically allowed (or willed) this particular child to be murdered. No parent who follows the tradition can help thinking that God can control if God wants to control. Nor can parents help thinking about those children who are hated and abused by their parents, whose young minds are already sick from such abuse and neglect, and who will live to an adulthood which can only be filled with violence and grief. How do parents stop themselves from asking about a divine wisdom which willed (permitted) my child, full of love and grace, to be the particular means to demonstrate the general truth that a just, loving God will punish a society which permits injustices?

C. S. Lewis had been for thirty years a thoughtful and deeply committed Christian. Yet, in his late fifties, he nearly lost his faith when his wife died from cancer. Lewis had earlier argued that all have sinned in Adam and, therefore, all stand guilty before God. But in the wake of his wife's death, he discovered that without a particular justification for that particular death he fell into rebellion against God.

> If God's goodness is inconsistent with hurting us, then either God is not good or there is no God: for in the only life we know He hurts us beyond our worst fears and beyond all we can imagine. If it is consistent with hurting us, then He may hurt us after death as unendurably as before it. (Lewis, *Grief*, p. 25.)

In time, Lewis recovered his faith in a loving God. The thought that came with the recovery was that his wife's death was God's way of showing him how weak his faith was; it was "sent to try him," though he cautions us to take "sent to try" in the right way.

> God has not been trying an experiment on my faith or love in order to find out their quality. He knew it already. It was I who didn't. In this trial He makes us occupy the dock, the witness box, and the bench all at once. He always knew that my temple was a house of cards. His only way of making me realize the fact was to knock it down. (Lewis, *Grief*, pp. 42–43.)

Lewis struggles here to regain his peace of mind and stay within the bounds of the tradition. God is understood as a loving parent hurting him in order to help him mature; his suffering is the consequence of his sin, for it is due to his inadequate faith; his faith's inadequacy could not be recognized until his wife's "God-sent" death knocked it down.

There is nothing false about Lewis's recovery of his faith; it was apparently brought about by a strong sense of his wife's presence and of God's. His theological resolution, however, raises some questions for it leaves too many loose ends. For example, his wife's death was sent to try his faith, not hers; she apparently accepted her dying without a crisis of faith. Her death, then, has a constructive meaning in his life, but what meaning did it have for her and for those close to her, particularly her two adolescent sons? (The marriage was Lewis's first, but her second; her children were living with them.) Her sons had already suffered separation from their father through divorce; they now were suffering the loss of their mother, presumably—can we draw any other conclusion?—because God had no other way to deal with their stepfather's inadequate "house of cards" faith. Nowhere does Lewis's keen mind reflect on this aspect of the matter. He does argue that the marriage had reached perfection and that it had no further reason to be prolonged. God, he says, is like a teacher who "moves you on": when "you have learned to do quadratics and enjoy doing them you will not be set them much longer." (Lewis, *Grief*, p. 40.) Still, we need to ask ourselves from whose viewpoint had the marriage no further reason to be prolonged? Surely not the children's, for they had to live now without their mother and with a stepfather who increasingly withdrew from life, lost his good health, and died within three years of his wife's death.

Simone Weil, the French religious writer, has said that "when one finds a comforting reply, first of all one has constructed it oneself." It is hard to gauge how much comfort Lewis drew from his "house of cards" reply. It may be that what little peace he found in his last years came more from the intimations of immortality that he hinted at than from the theological reply he advanced. Still, Lewis knew he needed the theological reply; immortal life, in itself, cannot justify an unjustified action in mortal life. But the reply, which Lewis constructed, depends on the questionable assumption that his faith was inadequate. It also forces him to turn his marriage and wife into "means" towards the "end" of his maturing faith and leads him to liken his married life to the learning of a quadratic equation. Did Lewis really believe this about his marriage? Do we? More troubling is his refusal, at least in the journal where he is thinking theologically, to raise the question of the meaning of his wife's death for the two boys. Was it merely the self-concern induced by his grief that prevented him from this consideration, or did he instinctively know that to open that Pandora's box would release a host of questions that would undo the theological reply he had given himself?

The tradition recognizes that the problem of evil finally poses more questions than answers, more windows than storm windows. At its outermost edge the tradition calls a halt to its attempts to explain evil or justify God. It admits, as Lewis will not, that there are events which defy all our attempts to discover any divinely hidden meaning or purpose in them. It asks us to see evil ultimately not as a problem which faith can solve but as an insoluble mystery which we can only encounter with faith. We are at that point in the tradition where theological justification gives way to mystery.

To help us understand the tradition's invocation of mystery, I turn not to a theological work but to Camus's novel *The Plague.* We find here a powerful, dramatic expression of faith encountering evil. The action of the novel takes place in an Algerian city struck by bubonic plague and under quarantine. The plague is claiming more than 500 victims a week.

Contrasted to each other are the humanist, Dr. Rieux, and the orthodox, Father Paneloux. Rieux devotes himself to fighting

the plague; he spends his waking moments tending the sick, running
the hospital, persuading others to join a volunteer band of workers
who gather up the dead, bury them, and keep the houses and streets
as sanitary as possible. Rieux has no need to find ulterior meaning
in the outburst of plague; he sees it as caused by long dormant bacilli
which, obedient to laws of nature, periodically erupt. They
uncaringly, senselessly spread their death-dealing power into the
bodies of living creatures, first rats and then humans. Rieux has
long ago abandoned belief in any divine reality. He gives his life to
help others because, in a universe filled with forces hostile and alien
to life, only human beings can care for and value each other.

    Father Paneloux is prophet and priest to the plague-stricken
city. We first meet him at the time of the initial outbreak of the
plague. He is preaching a prophetic sermon on the need for
repentance. The plague, he says, is a scourge of God brought about
by the people's religious indifference. The people are morally
apathetic and spiritually anemic; they give only token adherence to
Christian beliefs. God has long looked for an active Christian life of
love, but not finding it, has withdrawn from the city. In the absence
of God's compassionate presence and light "the thick darkness of
this plague" comes. The plague is not to be interpreted simply as
punishment for sin, for it contains within it a message of comfort
and love. It has the power to rouse us from our faithless slumbers
and point us to the path of salvation. The righteous have no need to
fear it.

    We find in this sermon the themes of the tradition. God is
love and power where power means control. God is an independent
reality and can withdraw from us at will. Evil is punishment for sin
but is also an occasion for self-knowledge, repentance, and
deepened faith. God inflicts suffering on us and lets us suffer
because there is no other way to heal us.

    The plague continues. Paneloux moves out of his study and
into the houses of stricken people; he feels the suffering of the ill
and grief-stricken. He stops talking about divine punishment and
joins Rieux's band of sanitary workers who are risking their own
lives in trying to limit the spread of the bacilli. There is a crucial
scene where Paneloux joins Dr. Rieux at the bedside of a stricken
little boy. Rieux has injected a new anti-plague serum into the child

and now they are waiting to see if it will take effect. The boy tosses convulsively on his bed; his agony goes on for hours. Paneloux realizes that the serum may have simply allowed the child to resist death longer. He says, "So if he is to die, he will have suffered longer." Finally, the boy opens his mouth and utters a long, seemingly endless wail of pain. Paneloux kneels and prays, "My God, spare this child." The boy's screams continue. Suddenly they cease. He is dead.

Rieux walks out of the room. Paneloux follows and tries to stop him. Rieux turns on Paneloux and says, "Ah, that child anyway was innocent, and you know it as well as I do." Paneloux responds, "What we've been seeing was as unbearable to me as it was to you. . . . That sort of thing is revolting because it passes our human understanding. But perhaps we should love what we cannot understand." Rieux, echoing Dostoevsky's Ivan, says, "No Father, I've a very different idea of love. And until my dying day I shall refuse to love a scheme of things in which children are put to torture." To which the priest answers, "Ah, Doctor, I've just realized what is meant by grace."

Shortly thereafter, Paneloux preaches a second sermon. His judgmental voice is gone, his topic is grace. Grace is being able to love God even when we cannot understand how a loving God allows the innocent to suffer. The agonizing cries of a child in the throes of death are unbearable to us; yet, since God assents to it, we must assent to it. We are being sorely tried here, but we must "believe everything so as not to be forced into denying everything." We must believe that all things issue from divine love. We cannot say, "this I understand, but that I cannot accept. . . . We must hold fast trusting in the divine goodness." As for what we should do, "We must do what good lies in our power" even at the cost of our own health or life.

Paneloux is no longer the prophet interpreting God's destructive power for us. He is not even a C. S. Lewis desperately searching for some rationale, for some meaning, to these events. He has given up on finding meanings or reasons for terrible sufferings. He is now a fellow-sufferer trying to hang on, like the rest of us, to his faith. He has stopped asking why God is doing these things; he is now asking how he can maintain his faith in the face of what he believes God is doing. He has had to shift his question because his understanding has come to the end of its tether. He can no longer see reasons; instead, the reason with which he sees threatens to break his belief in a divine reality whom he understands either as all-powerful and loving or as nothing. Therefore, he urges his congregation, and himself, to "believe everything so as not to be forced into denying everything." If we do not believe that everything reflects God's loving, just decrees, then we shall lose our sense of security, order and meaning in things. Chance or randomness will appear to us as ruler of the universe. Here Paneloux is at one with Lewis, who fought so hard to find a godly reason for his wife's death. Like all of us, Lewis wants his life and his world to make sense. In order to bring his wife's death into a pattern of meaning, he is willing to strain the credulity of the reader and, perhaps, even his own. Paneloux, faced with a greater horror, is not abandoning the belief that all events fit into a pattern of meaning; he is abandoning the belief that he can understand how all events fit into a pattern of meaning.

What ultimately matters for Paneloux is not that we understand the sense of things but that we have faith in the sense of things. Since understanding fails us when we encounter the suffering of the innocent, we must rely on the grace of God for our faith. It is no wonder that as Paneloux leaves the child's death bed, he says he has just understood the meaning of grace. Grace is loving a loving God when our experience will not let us understand God as loving. Grace is believing there is meaning in the very events which destroy the meanings we construct.

Our discussion has come to the outer edge of the tradition; this is the place where human reason and human experience suffer humiliation in order to allow for faith. It is also the place where the Catholic tradition, represented by Paneloux, meets the Protestant tradition.

Protestantism begins with Luther's insistence that we are saved by faith alone through grace. Luther is not only interested in humbling our reason but in vilifying it. Reason, for Luther, inexorably leads us to unbelief. The Protestant tradition, therefore, has tended to be more suspicious of reason than Catholic tradition. But on the far edge of faith where the experience of extreme evil and suffering takes us, the Catholic sense of the limits of reason approaches the Protestant distrust of reason. Paneloux's declaration that we must love and assent to what we cannot understand reminds us of Barth's assertion that the experience of faith affirms what in logic may be an absolute contradiction. Even more than Paneloux, Barth is unwilling to grant reason the authority to deprive us of the "securing" power of an all-controlling deity.

And yet, Barth finally moves away from the notion that God is all-controlling. Despite all that he had said earlier about faith requiring us to affirm everything as included in the good, in the end Barth acknowledges the genuine power of evil and the limits of God's power in relation to evil. Until Barth, the tradition had sought to contain evil within God's power by thinking of evil as necessary for some greater good or as permitted by God to allow for human freedom. It ignored the argument that some evils were so great that they could only signify sheer wreckage and that not even human freedom could account for or justify them. But in Barth the tradition takes a new turn. It corrects itself by going beyond itself. It responds to the question of evil by hinting at real limits in God, not self-limits, but limits imposed on God by the nature of reality. The way that Barth acknowledges these limits involves a somewhat technical, somewhat tortured, though highly original, discussion.

In *Church Dogmatics,* Barth begins his discussion on evil and divine power with a straightforward endorsement of the traditional idea of the all-controlling nature of divine power. (Barth, *Dogmatics,* III, 3, pp. 3ff.) He interprets God's sovereignty and Lordship as God's control over our independent acts. Though we experience evil and suffering, we know that God is good. Therefore we must take on faith that the world is good and that nothing, in fact, is excluded from the good. It is only our limited perspective that prevents us from seeing that.

These points remind us that Barth intends to be the voice of the living tradition in the twentieth century. All his inclinations are to present a strong, unambiguous defense of the theological tradition. Yet at the conclusion of that defense he opens a new discussion on the reality and origin of evil, introduces the concept of Nothingness, and intimates that God cannot prevent the occurrence of evil. (Barth, *Dogmatics,* III, 3, pp. 289–368.)

Barth moves beyond the traditional idea that we are to think of reality simply in terms of the creator and the creature. He says that we must recognize a third factor called Nothingness. Nothingness is a power which is absolutely alien to the creation. It is opposed to all that is good, it can and does affect us, and we can see its presence in sin, death, and destructive suffering. Yet Barth is not falling into a new form of dualism. Nothingness does not have its origin apart from God; it owes its reality indirectly to God's power. God intends the goodness of creation and says "yes" to that goodness. But that very "yes" implies a "no," the evil which God rejects. Barth's argument is that even God's "no" is sufficient to give Nothingness its reality. Nothingness, then, is God's negative or anti-creation which inevitably, tragically, arises in the wake of the positive creation.

Here is the pathos of the tradition. Its long travail to deny the possibility that any reality lies outside the good will and purpose of God has here come to its end. Barth calls Nothingness the impossible possibility. It must be impossible because (the nature of) divine control forbids it. It must be possible because there is genuine evil. There is senseless suffering, suffering from which no good issues, suffering without reason or purpose. The tension between what must be possible and what must be impossible strains the tradition and cracks it. Something gives in the notion of divine control. What other conclusion can we draw from Barth's analysis? God's own power to create entails a certain powerlessness. God runs into a real limit in relation to the occurrence of evil in the creation. God cannot say "yes" to goodness without bringing the "no" of evil into existence.

Is Barth suggesting that God is helpless to prevent evil? "Helpless" is perhaps too melodramatic or emotion-laden, but it does suggest the sense of the tragic character of the creation and of a tragic side to God as creator. We cannot have a world without evil, and God cannot create a world without simultaneously creating what is alien and hostile to that world. God pays a tragic price for creation just as we pay a tragic price for existence. Limits come with the creation. These limits are not simply apparent limits. Nothingness is intended to suggest the genuine power of evil; and these are not self-limits. God as creator lacks the power to prevent the existence of or to annihilate Nothingness.

What kind of concept is Nothingness? Is it philosophic, symbolic, poetic, technical, metaphoric? Barth's genius uses terms to suit his purposes even though such usage defies normal meanings and normal categories. He uses Nothingness, I would say, to put a gentle, subtle end to a two-thousand-year-old tradition of the all-controlling power of God. Why he takes the tradition around this turn, is, of course, a matter of speculation. He had no intellectual problem affirming both human freedom and absolute divine control, so it is not a matter of his bowing to the authority of logic. Perhaps the answer lies closer to home, to our existential home, in the twentieth century. Barth was a German-speaking, German-educated Swiss. He saw Hitler's rise to power; he knew close up the brutality of Nazism, and he knew Dachau, Auschwitz, and Buchenwald. He must have felt deeply God's "no" to what had been until then the humanly unimaginable horrors of the death camp. God said "no," and yet it happened. Barth needed to explain theologically how the Holocaust could happen.

This discussion of the problem of evil has taken us to the breaking edge of the tradition. In Barth's concept of Nothingness it takes us beyond the point of believing in divine purposes and meanings in *every* horror, no matter how great. It acknowledges that evil is genuine, freedom is real, and that there are real limits to God's power. It suggests that there are factors apart from and opposed to God which affect decisions and actions, and these factors are not controlled by God nor are they part of an eternal divine plan. To say all this constitutes the beginning of a revolution in our understanding of God and the problem of evil.

We need to ask three questions about these statements. First, are they biblical? Do they lie inside the bounds of biblical faith, even though they are outside the theological tradition? Second, are they conceivable? Can we conceive of God with limits? Does such a notion make sense? Third, are they christological? Do they allow us to affirm Christ's redemptive power over evil? These questions set the agenda for the following three chapters.

3

Mining the Seams
of the Bible

It was Whitehead who defined youth as life untouched by
tragedy. But then some are not young for very long. One of those is
Russell Baker, the columnist and wry humorist of the *New York
Times*. What follows is an account of that moment in his life when
his young cousins find the five-year-old Baker playing in the woods
and blurt out the news that his father is dead.

"Your father's dead," Kenneth said.
It was like an accusation that my father had done something criminal
and I came to my father's defense.
"He is not," I said.
But of course they didn't know the situation. I started to explain. He
was sick. In the hospital. My mother was bringing him home right
now. . . .
"He's dead," Kenneth said.
His assurance slid like an icicle into my heart.
"He is not either!" I shouted.
"He is too," Ruth Lee said. "They want you to come home right away."
I started running up the road screaming, "He is not!" It was a weak
argument. They had the evidence as I hurried home crying, "He is
not . . . he is not . . . he is not. . . ." I was almost certain before I got
there that he was.

And I was right. Arriving at the hospital that morning my mother was told he had died at 4:00 a.m. in "acute diabetic coma." He was 33 years old. When I came running home, my mother was still not back from Frederick, but the women had descended on our house, as women there did in such times, and were already busy with the housecleaning and cooking that were Morrisonville's ritual response to death. With a thousand tasks to do, they had no time to handle a howling five-year-old. I was sent to the opposite end of town to Bessie Scott's house. Poor Bessie Scott. All afternoon she listened patiently as a saint while I sat in her kitchen and cried myself out. For the first time I thought seriously about God. Between sobs I told Bessie that if God could do things like this to people, then God was hateful and I had no more use for Him.

Bessie told me about the peace of Heaven and the joy of being among the angels and the happiness of my father who was already there. This argument failed to quiet my rage. "God loves us just like His own children," Bessie said. "If God loves me why did he make my father die?"

Bessie said I would understand someday, but she was only partly right. That afternoon, though I couldn't have phrased it this way then, I decided that God was a lot less interested in people than anybody in Morrisonville was willing to admit. That day I decided that God was not entirely to be trusted. After that I never cried again with any real conviction, nor expected much of anyone's God except indifference, nor loved deeply without fear that it would cost me deeply in pain. At the age of five I had become a skeptic and began to sense that any happiness that came my way might be the prelude to some grim, cosmic joke. (Russell Baker, *Growing Up*, [New York: Congdon and Weed, 1982], pp. 61–62.)

Baker lost more than his father that day. His tragic experience cost him his childhood and his faith in a beneficent deity. He was only a five-year-old when his father died but there was nothing childlike in his "sense that any happiness that came my way might be the prelude to some grim, cosmic joke." He had not ceased believing in God, he had ceased believing that God was to be trusted. Baker had decided, and apparently nothing later in life shook him out of that decision, that "God was a lot less interested in people than anybody in Morrisonville was willing to admit."

Baker's decision regarding God's character seems to place him beyond the pale of biblical faith. Yet it is remarkable how much, both in tone and in content, his dialogue with Bessie Scott

evokes an earlier dialogue, this time a biblical one, by a writer who
must have shared Baker's sense that life has that about it which feels
like a "grim, cosmic joke."

> Though I am innocent, I cannot answer him . . .
> For he crushes me with a tempest,
>   and multiplies my wounds without cause;
> he will not let me get my breath,
>   but fills me with bitterness. . . .
> I am blameless . . . therefore I say,
>   he destroys both the blameless and the wicked.
> When disaster brings sudden death,
>   he mocks at the calamity of the innocent.
>   (Job 9:15–23)

The words, of course, are Job's; they were written almost
twenty-five hundred years ago by an Israelite who came to question
what he once deeply believed. In its portrait of Job, the Bible offers
us "a blameless and upright man" whose encounter with tragedy
leads him to repudiate an ancient tradition which heretofore had
guided and comforted him. That tradition, passed down in Israel in
both written and oral form, accounted for human suffering with the
theory that only the guilty suffer. In the book of Job this traditional
explanation of evil is put into the mouths of the three friends who
come to comfort Job after they hear of his suffering.

The first of Job's friends or comforters asks him, "Who that
is innocent ever perished?" (4:7) and advises him to "despise not
the chastening of the Almighty" (5:17). The second friend suggests
that Job is being punished for the sins of his children (8:4), and the
third assures Job "that God exacts of you less than your guilt
deserves" (11:6). But Job no more accepts the explanations of his
friends Eliphaz the Temanite, Bildad the Shuhite, and Zopher the
Naamathite than Baker accepted the explanation of Bessie Scott
of Morrisonville.

Baker knew, as Job knew, that he did not deserve his
suffering, and that a loving God would not have decreed or allowed
his father to die. The five-year-old boy knew this with an immediacy
that was so intense that neither adult authority nor religious
tradition could wither its certainty. And later reflection seems only

to have reinforced this conviction despite the fact that Baker, like Job, prospered in his life after his calamity. Baker went on to college, married, had children, and has pursued a remarkably successful career as a nationally syndicated journalist.

But Baker's life parts from Job's at a crucial point. Job, the questioner, is vindicated by God and the religious community. The defenders of the tradition, Job's comforters, are condemned. In Baker's case, however, skeptical questions alienate him from God and from the religious community (which continued to embody the tradition he had come to question). There is nothing in Baker's life story that parallels God's condemnation of the three friends for not having "spoken of me what is right, as my servant Job has" (42:7).

If we ask ourselves why Baker remained alienated while Job was able to overcome his alienation, we do not come up with any simple answer. Job repents; that is, he turns away from his alienated relation to God after being addressed twice by God out of the whirlwind. But we must pay careful attention to the speech of God in these addresses. Neither address attempts to account for Job's suffering or for the presence of suffering in human life. Instead, Job is simply reminded of God's mighty, creative works: the sea, the light, the winds, the stars, the rain, the lion, the wild ox, the horse. Even the mighty monsters, Behemoth and Leviathan, symbols of chaos and evil, are God's creatures and owe all their powers to God. God asks Job:

> "Will you condemn me that you may be justified?
> Have you an arm like God,
>   and can you thunder with a voice like his?" (Job 40:8–9)

After standing silent before God's two speeches, Job finally responds:

> "I have uttered what I did not understand,
>   things too wonderful for me,
>   which I did not know . . .
> I had heard of thee by the hearing of the ear,
>   but now my eye sees thee;
> therefore I despise myself,
>   and repent in dust and ashes." (Job 42:3–6)

There are two possible interpretations of this speech. The most obvious one is that Job has simply given up. He has not received any answers to his questions, but he comes to recognize the impossibility of his position before God. His confrontation with God, the Creator of the universe, dramatizes his own impotence and insignificance in the great scheme of things. Who is he, a mere mortal, to raise questions about God's use of power? As the voice out of the whirlwind reminds him, he neither has "an arm like God," nor can he "thunder with a voice like his" (40:9).

But if we follow this interpretation we need to ask whether Job "gives up" out of a sense of wrongness in questioning God or because he thinks that it is futile to do so. Whichever answer we give we run into difficulties. We cannot say that Job was wrong in raising questions since the voice out of the whirlwind has already declared that Job has "spoken of me what is right." If we answer that it is futile to raise questions of justice with God, we undermine the essential role of justice in Israel's faith. The justice of God was always as significant to Israel as the power of God. To cut God's power off from questions of justice would leave us with a God worshiped only for the awe that power inspires. But this is impossible for Israel. If Israel knows God at all, she knows God as just.

There is another interpretation, popular for some time now among theologians, which holds that Job acted correctly in raising the question of divine justice. In this view, Job's friends erred in allowing an ideology—only the guilty suffer—to override the experience of undeserved suffering. Job knows that his suffering is undeserved. What he does not know is how it is possible for undeserved suffering to occur. That question remains unanswered. But he does experience God's holy and healing presence. He discovers that in the presence of God's love, his complaints can find their resting place. His pain is stilled and he attains "a state of mind in which there is no desire to ask" about the justice of God. The experience of God's love has proven sufficient to him: "Now my eye sees thee." It is enough. All else appears superfluous. Therefore, he repents—that is, he turns away from that state of mind which needs to question God. (The quote and the interpretation are from

William Temple, *Nature, Man and God*, [London: Macmillan, 1934], p. 43; cf. also S. Terrien, "Job" *Interpreter's Bible*, III, p. 902. This interpretation has achieved such currency that it has worked its way into the footnote to Job 42:1–6 in *The New Oxford Annotated Bible* RSV.)

These are two different interpretations. The first moves toward a God awesome in might and power; the second moves toward a God of grace and love. Yet the two have something in common: they both stop the argument about evil. This is obvious in the first interpretation where it is either futile or wrong to argue about the relation of power to justice. But even the second interpretation suggests that while it was right and perhaps even necessary in the sixth century B.C. to question God's justice, it is no longer necessary or even right to continue to do so. Job may compare God to a lion hunting its prey (10:16) or to a taskmaster over slaves (3:18) or accuse God of multiplying his wounds without cause (9:17). But because we have come to know God as graciously present in our suffering, such accusations now seem to be inappropriate for faith. Today those who would speak the words of Job, like Russell Baker, see themselves and are seen by others as having placed themselves outside biblical faith.

There are, however, some signs that we are changing our minds on that score. Elie Wiesel, the Jewish novelist and survivor of the Nazi death camps has faulted Job for cutting off his argument with God. Even if Job does experience divine grace, Wiesel does not think the experience of God's love should obscure God's concern for justice. In ancient Israel, God was proclaimed as having a passion for justice. Indeed, Israel's passion for justice was rooted in God's passion. The prophetic demand for justice did not arise out of some high ethical ideal, but out of the understanding of God's nature as just. When Job calls God to account, he does so not on the basis of a human ideal but on the basis of Israel's knowledge of God's own nature. Wiesel, therefore, insists that we too must take the early Job as our model. We must continue to call God to account. We must even bring God to trial. We do so not out of human arrogance, but out of biblical faith. The God of the Bible has been revealed to us as just, and we must be vigilant about that justice.

We are left with two questions: Does Job stop questioning God because divine grace gives him rest, stills his pain, and makes questions of justice appear superfluous? Or are questions of God's justice ones which a biblical community is continually called to ask?

The odd thing about biblical texts is that they never seem to allow us to rest with the meanings we give them. They have a way of forcing us to go back to them and struggle some more. Let us return to the text in order to complete the story. We are told that the "Lord blessed the latter days of Job more than his beginning." He had twice as many camels, oxen and asses as he had before and ten more children were born to him. He "saw his sons, and his sons' sons, four generations. And Job died, an old man, and full of days" (42:12–17).

The text tells us that Job was given more than he had. But it does not tell us that Job felt the birth of new children justified the death of his first set of children. Job lived to be an old man, "full of days." But there is nothing in the text that stops us from thinking that on any one of those days, or even on all of those days, Job might awaken with the memory of one of his dead children in his head and bitter tears on his face. Wiesel may be correct. The earlier experience of God's grace might not stop Job from shouting, once again, that God is more like a lion hunting his prey than like a just ruler of a kingdom. Of course, the text tells us nothing of this. But we imagine what it would be like for us, and we listen to those other voices in Scripture which do not allow the experience of grace to shut off the questions of divine justice. The psalmist cries:

> Thou hast made us like sheep for the slaughter,
>   and hast scattered us among the nations . . .
> All this has come upon us,
>   though we have not forgotten thee,
>   or been false to thy covenant. (44:11–17)

Has there ever been a time when this cry has not been true for some person or some people somewhere? Perhaps the book of Job is trying to tell us not that it sees a way through the problem of evil but that it sees through the answers we have used to comfort ourselves. The Bible responds profoundly to the deepest problems of life and faith but that does not mean that the Bible has one answer, or a final answer, or even consistent answers to the problem of God, power, and evil.

We have a tendency, sometimes, to think of Scripture as if it were a train on a single track heading determinedly for its final destination. But the Bible is not really like that. Perhaps the Bible is more like a deep coal mine with many seams, some of which are rich with coal, others are not. Some when pursued seem to be endless, and others when pursued become thinner and thinner.

If we think of the Bible as a coal mine with seams we have been mining for centuries and others we have hardly touched, then we have our clue to how a view of God other than that of the main theological tradition can also be a biblical view. The theological tradition has mined one of the large seams in Scripture. Let us call that seam the monarchial image. In this seam, God is a great, awesomely mysterious and powerful Creator. He is a loving and just King. All-controlling and all-knowing, nothing happens outside his will. He never changes in any way; he is eternally the same. He especially never changes his mind.

We are all familiar with this image of God. It is the one with which most of us have been brought up. It is also the one that troubles our faith when we ask how can God allow so much senseless human suffering to occur.

There is no question that Scripture contains an extensive seam to which this image of God can trace its origins. As we saw in the book of Job, the monstrous Behemoth and Leviathan are considered playthings of God (40:15–41:34). Job himself declares, "I know that thou canst do all things, and that no purpose of thine can be thwarted" (42:2). In the book of Isaiah, God says, "I form light and create darkness, I make weal and create woe [the Hebrew word is rācāh, more accurately translated in the King James Version as "evil"], I am the Lord who do all these things" (45:7). In the fourth Gospel, Jesus says to Pilate, "You would have no power over me unless it had been given you from above" (John 19:11), and in the Gospel according to Matthew, Jesus declares, "With God all things are possible" (19:26). In Romans, Paul writes that God "has mercy upon whomever he wills, and he hardens the hearts of whomever he wills" (9:18). In Acts, we are told that Jesus was crucified "according to the definite plan and foreknowledge of God" (2:23). In the book of Jeremiah, God says, "Before I formed you in the womb I knew you, and before you were born I consecrated you" (1:5). Job declares that God "is unchangeable and who can turn him?" (23:13). In Malachi, God says, "for I the Lord do not change" (3:6), and James states that in God "there is no variation or shadow due to change" (1:17).

This is an extensive seam and we are all familiar with it. Its view of God has impressed itself upon the mind of the theological tradition and the imagination of the church. It is the image that Baker knew. But there are other seams in the Bible, seams which run toward a different image of God. This image has been barely explored because the monarchial image was so strongly established. The monarchial image seemed to have riches deep enough to meet our needs.

Dietrich Bonhoeffer, the German pastor and theologian executed by the Nazis in 1945 for his involvement in the plot to assassinate Hitler, portrayed an alternative image in the following lines written from his prison cell:

> Men go to God when they are sore bestead,
> Pray to him for succour, for his peace, for bread,
> For mercy for them sick, sinning, or dead;
> All men do so, Christian and unbelieving.
>
> Men go to God when he is sore bestead,
> Find him poor and scorned, without shelter or bread,
> Whelmed under weight of the wicked, the weak, the dead;
> Christians stand by God in his hour of grieving.
>
> God goes to every man when sore bestead,
> Feeds body and spirit with his bread;
> For Christians, pagans alike he hangs dead,
> And both alike forgiving. (Dietrich Bonhoeffer, *Letters and Papers from Prison*, [London: SCM, 1953], pp. 348–49.)

Here is an image of God which runs against the notion of an unchanging, controlling, awesomely powerful, predestinating planner. It is an image which seems to emerge when members of a faithful community are overwhelmed by the experience of evil and undeserved suffering. Bonhoeffer's thoughts from a Nazi prison break traditional modes of thinking in a way similar to Barth's concept of Nothingness. Here, God is imaged with real limits: "whelmed under weight of the wicked," grieving, weak by worldly standards and conceptions, and going out to us in suffering and forgiveness. This is the image of the vulnerable God. Of course, it is but an image. We need to fill it out, ask questions of it, and think systematically about it. But first we need to find the seam in the Bible to which it corresponds and which nourished it, sometimes hiddenly, all these years.

Let us begin not so much with ideas of God in the Bible, or even pictures of God, but with the tone of God. In the texts that follow there is not only passion in God's voice, there is the tone of vulnerability:

> "Is Ephraim my dear son?
>   Is he my darling child?
> For as often as I speak against him,
>   I do remember him still.
> Therefore my heart yearns for him." (Jer. 31:20)

In Micah, Israel's stubborn faithlessness drives God to plead "before the mountains":

> "O my people, what have I done to you?
>   In what have I wearied you? Answer me!" (Mic. 6:3)

In Isaiah, there is wrathful passion:

> Woe to you, destroyer,
>   who yourself have not been destroyed;
>   you treacherous one. (Isa. 33:1)

The passionate tone of wrath is heard again in the scorn that Jesus pours on the scribes and Pharisees:

> "Woe to you, scribes and Pharisees, hypocrites . . . you . . . out-
> wardly appear beautiful . . . but within you are full of hypocrisy and
> iniquity." (Matt. 23:27–28)

There is the undertone of pain in Jesus' wrathful words as he enters the temple grounds and overthrows the tables of the money-changers:

> "It is written, 'My house shall be called a house of prayer'; but you have made it a den of robbers." (Matt. 21:13)

In Genesis, the murder of Abel immediately provokes a horrified outcry from God:

> "What have you done? The voice of your brother's blood is crying to me from the ground." (Gen. 4:10)

These lines are but a sampling of what we can think of as the seam of divine vulnerability in the Bible. The passion in them suggests that God is not only involved with but affected by—vulnerable to—the thoughts and actions of a people. What Israel does matters to God and has consequences for God. Also, God's passion is of a particular sort: it is that of moral outrage and disappointed love. There is little basis for the old interpretation that the high ethic in the Bible had been developed by a few prophets who were guided by lofty, moral principles. That was surely a mistaken view. Wickedness, hypocrisy, treachery, callousness are denounced by the prophet not because such ways of being assault some high principle, but because they are received or felt as assault by a just God. Yet God is not a ruthless moralist who judges without mercy. God is more than justice, more than the power of moral principles; God is also a lover. Hosea portrays God not as an invulnerable judge, but as a loving husband who feels the pain of his wife's (Israel's) harlotry (2:1–13), or as a betrayed father who suffers from his son's (Israel's) abandonment (11:1–4). God is caught in a struggle between the bonds of love and the binds of justice. Justice demands the destruction of the faithless Israel but God does not act out of justice alone. There is pathos in God's response because Israel is the beloved one:

> How can I give you up, O Ephraim!
> How can I hand you over, O Israel! . . .
> My heart recoils within me,
> my compassion grows warm and tender.
> I will not execute my fierce anger. (Hos. 11:8–9)

In Jeremiah there is the sure sense that Israel deserves the national disaster that is surely coming upon her (4:10). Yet here too God cries out in agony over the prospective destruction of the nation:

> My anguish, my anguish! I writhe in pain!
> Oh, the walls of my heart! (Jer. 4:19)

The translators of the RSV, by adding quotation marks to the original text, which has none, have sought to give the impression that the words of anguish are spoken by the prophet and not God. But the context clearly indicates that lines 13 to 22 represent the voice of God. This is an example of how the image of God that we bring to our reading of the Bible literally affects what we see.

The long liturgical passage in Matthew condemning the scribes and pharisees ends with a divine lament and a metaphor of motherly love:

> "O Jerusalem, Jerusalem, killing the prophets and stoning those who are sent to you! How often would I have gathered your children together as a hen gathers her brood under her wings, and you would not!" (Matt. 23:37)

The words "and you would not" sound a plaintive note as does the image of a mother hen gathering her brood. There is sadness in these words and images, a sense of longing and of unfulfilled hope.

Similarly, there is pathos in Luke's description of Jesus' initial reaction to the sight of Jerusalem:

> And when he drew near and saw the city he wept over it, saying, "Would that even today you knew the things that make for peace!" (Luke 19:41–42)

So far, I am talking about the tone in these texts, but not merely the tone because tone evokes an image. The image is not that of an all-controlling, all-knowing monarch whose purposes and plans cannot be thwarted; nor that of the impassive judge who metes out due punishment; nor that of the tester of righteousness who plumbs, by trial, the authenticity of a person's faith. All these images can be found and have been found in the Bible. They have their own texts, their own seams, though they are not seams of equal richness. The texts that we have been considering evoke the image of vulnerability because they focus on God caught in the conflict of living out both love and justice. This loving God in the Bible has a passion for justice. This just God of the Bible is also known to us as loving. When we find texts in which these two come together in conflict, there we find texts which burst with the anguish of God.

It is the relation of love and justice to each other that accounts for God's vulnerability to suffering—and that three times over. God suffers from those who perpetuate injustice (the treacherous ones, the destroyers) as, analogously—but only analogously—a music lover suffers upon hearing music played off-key. God suffers with the victims of injustice as a loving wife suffers when her husband bears undeserved affliction. And God suffers with the punishment of the unjust as a loving father suffers even when his children are only getting their just deserts.

We sometimes think of love and justice in irreconcilable conflict with each other. Perhaps we conceive the matter only in terms of logic. Justice is impartial and love is biased, or justice condemns and love forgives. Or perhaps we think they are irreconcilable because we conceive them under contrary images. Justice is the impassive judge or ruthless moralist, and love is the tender-hearted parent or the "blind" lover. ("Blind" justice and "blind" love run to opposite meanings.)

The literature of the Bible is primarily narrative or poetic in form; it is not analytical or conceptual. Israel does not learn that God is just and loving through an analysis of the divine nature. Rather, Israel discovers herself rescued from slavery and given a moral code by the same God. The prophets do not analyze the dynamics of love and justice in God; they intuitively experience how love and justice feel in God in a given particular moment. In the line, "How can I give you up, O Ephraim?" love and justice are experienced together. The question of "giving up" arises out of the dynamics of justice. Israel has been morally and religiously faithless. She has not cared for the "widow" and "the poor," and she has pursued other gods. She deserves destruction. The "how can I" expresses God's loving commitment to Israel. God is bonded in love to His people.

We could say that love and justice together make God vulnerable. But it would be truer to say that love and justice can be together in God because God is vulnerable. When we allow the ideas of love and justice to form our basic images of God we come up with two contradictory images: the ruthlessly impartial judge and the tender-hearted parent. But when we begin with the image of the vulnerable God then we can see that love and justice come together in the pathos or anguish of God.

Once we have the image of the vulnerable God, we can better see and mine that seam in the Bible. God may be outraged by the murder of Abel, but Cain's fear that others will slay him evokes divine compassion and protection (Gen. 4:13–15). God may flood the world in response to human wickedness but the text carefully notes that God does so with regret and grief, and not out of anger and blind justice (Gen. 6:3–6). God insists that Israel worship one God alone, not because monotheism is philosophically correct, but because God is "jealous," i.e., God's being is vulnerable to Israel's faithless action (cf. Exod. 20:5; Josh. 24:19, passim). God's turning to the Israelites enslaved in Egypt was not a response to the objective knowledge of an exploited people but to the groans of a people and their cries for help.

> And the people of Israel groaned under their bondage, and cried out for help, and their cry under bondage came up to God. And God heard their groaning, and God remembered his covenant with Abraham, with Isaac, and with Jacob. (Exod. 2:23–24)

In this basic text, which lies at the origin of the nation Israel, the primary image of God is not that of an all-knowing, all-controlling King. It is that of one who hears and responds to groans and cries for help. It is an image of one who is vulnerable to human affliction.

Of course, the Exodus story also pictures God with plenty of controlling power. God sends the plagues upon the Egyptians, hardens the heart of Pharaoh, divides the waters of the sea to allow the fleeing Israelites to pass, and then brings those waters down upon the pursuing Egyptian chariots and horsemen.

The monarchial image is present in the book of Exodus. But it is not simply or consistently present. There is no text that suggests that God willed the Egyptian enslavement of Israel or that God's response to Israel's groanings was pre-planned or even that God foreknew that Moses would take leadership responsibilities. We are so used to attributing to God the kind of power which directs and controls events that we tend to miss the extent to which the biblical stories suggest the open and unsettled character of God's involvement with the world. For example, is there anything in the Genesis text which suggests that God willed or foreknew the way in which Eve and Adam would respond to the serpent's temptation or how Cain would deal with his jealousy of his brother or that wickedness would grow rampant by the time of Noah or that an Egyptian king would arise "who did not know Joseph?" (Exod. 1:8).

We could say that Israel thinks of God under both images. When she suffers from injustice, or even from divine judgment, she thinks of God as vulnerable and suffering with her. When she thinks of overcoming injustice or suffering, she thinks of God as an all-controlling King. This is a way of describing the dynamics of the Bible. But when we use it, have we settled our theological problem? Or does the tension between the opposing images indicate that the biblical testimonies press beyond themselves toward a more inclusive solution? Perhaps we need to think of biblical narratives as being on the way to understanding what kind of God we live under and call Lord.

Let us go back to Job. The monarchial image is clearly not working there. If the earlier biblical narratives testified to God as vulnerable to suffering but mighty in protecting the innocent sufferer, the book of Job testifies to the experience that God does not protect the weak and innocent. We could answer that God stands above our concepts of justice. That would save the monarchial image but it would undermine the central place that justice has in Israel's faith and would not resolve the problem of evil. Since the monarchial image is no longer functioning to resolve the problem of evil—indeed the opposite has become the case—the book of Job can be understood as questioning its adequacy. The problem is that the book of Job does not provide us with an alternative to the monarchial image. Or does it? Perhaps we never noticed because we have assumed that the monarchial image of God is as much a given in the text as it is in our mind.

There is a startling text toward the end of the book of Isaiah which throws light on our discussion:

> In all their affliction he [God] was afflicted,
>   and the angel of his presence saved them;
> in his love and in his pity he redeemed them. (Isa. 63:9)

(In the use of the word *afflicted,* the RSV translation is here following the suggested Masoretic reading of the Hebrew text. Similarly, Luther translates "as they were in dire straits so he [God] was in dire straits." Other readings of the ancient text lead to translations such as those in the NEB and the Jerusalem Bible.) The text dwells not on the monarchial power of God as the source of Israel's salvation, but on the tender elements in God which we associate with the image of vulnerability: affliction, saving presence, love and pity. Similarly, in the "suffering servant" passages the redemptive power of God is identified not by the attributes of monarchy but of vulnerability:

> The servant was despised and rejected by everyone,
>   was full of sorrows, and acquainted with grief, . . .
> Surely this one has borne our griefs
>   and carried our sorrows, . . .
> But this servant was wounded for our transgressions,
>   was bruised for our iniquities,
> bore the chastisement that made us whole
>   and the stripes by which we are healed. (Isa. 53:3–5;
> taken from *The Inclusive Language Lectionary*)

This passage speaks not of God's suffering but of the suffering of one sent by God. Even so, the text clearly relates suffering to redemptive power. It is as if the power of vulnerability now appears where once monarchial power appeared. In texts which we can date to the sixth century B.C., suffering is being understood not only as the consequence of God's love (as in the earlier texts of Israel's faith) but as the mode of God's redeeming power. But is it possible that this is also the case in the book of Job? (The story of Job as a "Knight" of faith who stays true to God despite calamities is an ancient Middle East folktale. The book of Job, as we have it, with its long poetic dialogues is generally dated to the mid-sixth century, certainly no earlier.) Certainly it would be difficult to justify an interpretation of Job as a suffering-servant figure, as an innocent one being punished for the sake of the guilty many. And yet we gain the clue into interpreting Job by asking ourselves why the suffering servant passages in Isaiah are so powerful for us.

Scholars have long noted that the origin of the notion of the suffering servant may lie in the ancient Middle East practice of sacrificing a "scapegoat" for our sins by driving one out into the wilderness to its certain death. Yet when *we* interpret the suffering servant passages we find their meaning not by looking back to the ancient notion of the sacrificial scapegoat, but by looking forward to the New Testament affirmation that God was in Christ, the crucified one who forgives us for our sins. When we read, "has borne our griefs . . . was wounded for our transgressions . . . and bore the stripes by which we are healed" we do not think backward to scapegoats but forward to Christ, the incarnate Word of God, whose suffering "makes us whole." The situation is not so much that the Isaiah passages prophesy the coming of Jesus Christ as it is that the fullness of their meaning has to wait upon a later event. The Isaiah passages are leading us toward a new understanding and image of God, specifically toward the image of a vulnerable God whose redemptive power lies in suffering with and for us. But we do not know that and could not say that until that new image appears through the words and actions of Jesus Christ. (This is, of course, a Christian reading of the Isaiah passages.)

Is there this kind of "leading to" in the book of Job? Quite the opposite seems to be the case. Dorothee Soelle calls the God who speaks out of the whirlwind a "pagan nature deity," by which she means that nothing but sheer power is being praised there. But this remark is a little misleading because it seems to forget that from the Joban point of view God's absolute power is at the heart of the problem of evil. Similarly, the answer that Job's experience of God's grace makes other issues superfluous is deceptive because it leads us away from Job's concern for God's justice. Neither God's speech of power and mystery nor the "happy ending" solve the problem of evil, not in the writer's mind and certainly not in the reader's. God's controlling power is part of the problem in the book of Job. Until that is confronted not even the experience of divine grace can account for Job's silence and repentance.

But what if the problem lies in *our* perspective? We are trying to understand Job by looking back to the monarchial image of God. We need to look at the book of Job in the same way that we look at the suffering-servant passages in Isaiah. We must interpret it in accordance with where it is leading us. Perhaps the book of Job will not make sense until we see it as turning away from the monarchial image of God and looking forward to a new image of God, namely, to God as vulnerable. Our failure to interpret Job forwardly, so to speak, makes us a little like Job's friends who cannot speak rightly about God because they cannot break away from earlier patterns of thinking.

Consider the fact that the speech of Elihu in ch. 37 is similar in substance to the speech that comes out of the whirlwind in ch. 38. Elihu praises God for his power, his thunderous voice, his wondrous works, and his incomprehensible ways. Further, he mocks Job as a weak, ignorant, arrogant human being who dares raise his voice against the terrible majesty of God. But this speech is placed in the mouth of the soon-to-be-condemned "friends." Its content is as suspect as any "friend's" speech. Thus, a shadow falls over the monarchial image of God at just that moment when the voice out of the whirlwind is about to assert it.

The speech out of the whirlwind is, of course, a ringing manifesto of divine power. But perhaps it rings too much—thirty-four lines about the monstrous Leviathan, twenty-four about Behemoth. The picture of divine power is so overdrawn that it raises questions about itself. Is it really an acceptable or even believable response to Job's questions about God's power and human suffering when the voice out of the whirlwind asks him:

> Have you an arm like God,
>   and can you thunder with a voice like his? (Job 40:9)

Is that an answer to a cry of pain?

The question is not simply whether the monarchial image is subtly being edged out. The question is also whether the book of Job is leading us toward a new image of God, an image of a suffering, vulnerable God. To answer that question, I need to return to some earlier ones. How can we account for Job's act of repentance? Of what does Job repent? When Job says, "Now my eye sees thee," what image of God does he see?

Let us begin with Job's description of what has happened to him:

> For the thing that I fear comes upon me,
> and what I dread befalls me. (Job 3:25)

The meaning of the text seems clear enough. Though Job had been a righteous and faithful servant of God, he still experienced fear and dread. The text sees nothing unusual in the coupling of faith and dread. It is likely that this coupling reflects the kind of under-standing of God and life present in the writer of Psalm 44:

> Thou hast made us like sheep for slaughter, . . .
> though we have not forgotten thee,
> or been false to thy covenant. (Ps. 44:11–17)

Faithfulness does not prevent the most terrible things from hap-pening. This is part of the experience of ancient Israel, particularly the Israel that in the sixth century B.C. suffered conquest and the destruction of its cities. When this experience is coupled with the monarchial image of an all-controlling God, there appears the God whom Job (and Baker) condemn. It is this God who is awesomely arbitrary by the standards of love and justice:

> Though I am innocent, I cannot answer [God] . . .
> For he crushes me with a tempest. (Job 9:15–17)

This kind of divine power is something to dread. But there is no indication in Job's speeches that it is God's power that he has come to dread. Nor is it his own death. We are told that Job longs for death, that he seeks it like hidden treasure and that he will be exceedingly glad to find his grave (3:21,22). Nor is it the loss of his children; that seems to be more the occasion for the dread than the dread itself.

The nature of his dread is suggested in a question Job asks:

> Why is light given to him that is in misery,
>   and life to the bitter in soul,
> who long for death, but it comes not? (Job 3:20–21)

The reference here is not to outer events but to an inner state. The terrible and tragic outer events have become the occasion for the dreadful inner event. Through no act of his own, and though he was without fault, Job has fallen among those who are embittered in soul and long for death. He continues to believe in God's existence, but he has come to loathe his life. Job has experienced death and loss in its many forms: his wealth and property destroyed, his children killed, his skin infected with sores. These are dreadful things but they are not yet dread.

Dread is despair at its furthermost point; it is, as Job says, having life where there is bitterness of soul. Dread is life which has come to hate itself; it is life turning against itself, becoming faithless to itself. It is, finally, life moving toward unfaith, unbelief at its most primal level. For when I dread the simple fact that I am alive, I deny, in the most basic way, the goodness of God's creation. There are many more destructive and evil ways to express rejection of God, but surely there are none that cut deeper into a person's life than to dread the fact of being alive.

Now we are ready to interpret Job's speech of repentance:

> I had heard of thee by the hearing of the ear,
>   but now my eye sees thee;
> therefore I despise myself,
>   and repent in dust and ashes. (Job 42:5–6)

Job repents, but his repentance comes after the healing. In that vision of God, "Now my eye sees thee," healing power was communicated. Job is healed of his hatred of life. He had fallen into dread, and now he is out of it. The loss of his children may still cause him anguish, but it no longer leads him into dread of life.

a bit far fetched

We come now to the crucial question. What kind of vision of God could bring about Job's healing? Surely the monarchial vision would not have this power. It might silence Job's outcry against unjust suffering, but it would not answer it. And it would not heal him of his bitterness of soul. As long as Job believes that God has all-controlling power, he has reason to believe that those who are crushed in life are crushed by God. But as we have seen, Elihu's speech and even the speech out of the whirlwind raise questions about the adequacy of that view of God. In raising those questions, the book of Job is leading us away from the monarchial image of God, and yet is leaving room for a new image of God to appear. Here is the clue into Job's healing and the content of his repentance.

Job is healed when a new image of God appears to him. Now he can let go of that monarchial image. He is healed because in letting go of that image of all-controlling power, he is letting go of the experience of God as the enemy. The "thee" that he sees in "Now my eye sees thee" is God the friend, the vulnerable one who suffers with him in his suffering and whose caring presence heals him. Job does not repent of his concern for unjust suffering; biblical faith can never do that. Job repents of his loathing for life, his sense of despair, his lack of faith in the goodness of the creation. Having turned away from despair, he is ready to return to life. He can now love again, work and have children. He can die, as the text says, "full of days."

Does this interpretation strain the text? The answer is yes and no. Yes, if we think of the book of Job as if its texts were without conflict, tension, and contradiction. The monarchial image is present in Job, and it is affirmed over and over again. But deliberately placed against it is the notion of undeserved suffering. The tension created by that placing must have been no less severe in the sixth century B.C., with all its violent upheavals, than it is for us when we place the slaughter of those in the Nazi death camps against the monarchial image of God.

Yet there is something in us that does not want to lose that monarchial image. We want to preserve it. Some of us reinterpret Job's character so that his life is not an example of undeserved suffering. We argue that Job is spiritually arrogant or does not know God's grace or that he needs to fall before he can experience the full joy of God's healing powers. But when we argue this way we want to eat our cake and have it too. For how can Job achieve peace of mind, no matter how much his fortunes are restored, as long as he thinks that it is God who crushes the innocent?

We can account for Job's "peace" by saying that in his experience of God in the whirlwind the vulnerable image of God appears, edging out the monarchial one. Of course, the subversion of the monarchial image and the affirmation of the vulnerable image can only occur indirectly. But that should not surprise us. It reflects the fact that the book of Job is written under the dual stress of existential pain and opposition to the dominant tradition.

We are left with the question, who is responsible for Job's suffering? Job was concerned about God's justice because he believed that God was wholly responsible for the events that caused his suffering. Are we now to say that God bears no responsibility whatsoever for evil?

I wish I could say that. For years I did believe that we could interpret the (alternative seam in the) Bible to show that God bears no responsibility for the wreckage and destruction in our life, that evil arises out of human freedom, or unjust social structures, or the instabilities of nature, or conflicting goods, or sheer chance. I thought that the image of the vulnerable God would allow us to dissociate God completely from evil because it allows us to conceive of God not as the cause of everything that is but as the source of all that is good and to be hoped for. I had personal reasons for wanting God clear of all responsibility for evil. The negative cornerstone of my faith was that God had no part in the death of my children. I feared that if the image of divine vulnerability did not succeed in divesting God of even partial or indirect responsibility for evil that my faith would become as Job's—embittered—or as Baker's—skeptical.

An essay by Camus gave me no peace on this issue. The topic of that essay was the incongruity of the human situation. We long for goodness and justice, yet we live in a world which inevitably frustrates these intense desires. Worse, there are none of us whose hands are completely clean. In a literary analysis of Matthew's text on "the murder of the innocents," Camus notes that not even Jesus could live his life apart from the guilt of shedding innocent blood. It is Christ's birth that occasions Herod's order to kill all male children under two in the city of Bethlehem.

Of course, Matthew did not intend to suggest that Christ bears any responsibility for the deaths of the infants of Bethlehem. He intended to demonstrate that Jesus was the Christ, the Son of God, by showing that the events surrounding Jesus' birth are all fulfillments of prophecy. But this does not affect the force of Camus's argument. Even an act of overwhelming goodness and innocence such as the birth of the Christ Child must bear responsibility for the pain and suffering which it occasions.

Certainly, we can muster evidence disputing the historicity of the "murder of the innocents." (Matthew is the only Gospel writer to mention it; Paul makes no reference to it, and the first-century Jewish historian, Josephus, who collected events depicting Herod's cruelty, makes no mention of any child massacre.) But this does not weaken the force of Camus's basic point. There remains the treachery of Judas, his suicide, the authorization of Jesus' death by the Jewish and Roman officials, the execution of Jesus by Roman soldiers: all these evils are occasioned by Jesus' life of love and goodness. It is, unfortunately, as true to say that Jesus shares in the responsibility for the evil his life occasioned in others as it is to say that Jesus is innocent of evil.

No matter how hard I tried, the question that Camus's essay lodged in the back of my head would not go away. Is it possible that even when we no longer conceive God under the image of monarchial power that God is still implicated in the evil that we suffer?

The issue was broken open for me by a question raised in a graduate seminar for ministers. We were discussing a sermon preached on the Cain-Abel text:

> . . . and the Lord had regard for Abel and his offering,
> but for Cain and his offering he had no regard.
> So Cain was very angry, and his countenance fell. (Gen. 4:4–5)

The stage is set for Cain to slay his brother out of envy that God took pleasure in Abel's offering but not in his. This is a disturbing text because it suggests that Cain's murder of Abel was triggered by the arbitrary character of God's decision-making. Commentators are uncomfortable with the text and have offered various interpretations to blunt its impact. One interpretation is that the fault is Cain's because he should have known of the necessity for a blood sacrifice. Another is that the story reflects not God's arbitrary choosing of Abel but the Israelite bias for the shepherd over that of the farmer. (Israelites were originally shepherds, while their early enemies, the Canaanites, were an agricultural people). Others seek to disarm the text by reminding us that we are dealing here not with historical events but with a primeval myth symbolizing the murderous road humanity has taken, the consequences of which cannot be undone in any simple way.

The argument that Cain, a tiller of the soil, would assume that blood sacrifice was a better expression of faith than "the fruit of the ground" finds no support in the text and strains our imagination. The other arguments have their point, but they pay the price of explaining away the issue of God's involvement, rather than facing the issue of divine responsibility which it raises. Martin Buber deals with this text by likening the Cain story to the testing of Abraham where God appears as the tester of righteousness. This is a helpful insight, but the parallel falters because things go awry in the Cain story. In the Abraham-Isaac story, the events are kept under God's control; in the Cain-Abel story, more seems to happen than was intended. Also, Buber is silent on the question of God's responsibility for Abel's death.

We were discussing these matters when one of the ministers, a director of a clinical-pastoral education program, asked whether God is involved with and responsible for evil. I thought these were two separate issues, so I responded with the question, "Are you asking whether God is involved with evil or whether God is responsible for evil?" He paused for a moment and answered, "Is God responsible because God is involved?"

That was it, of course. That was the answer to the distressing question that Camus's essay had lodged in my head. God is responsible because God is involved. There are not two issues but one. What is perhaps a truism in pastoral counseling becomes a startling insight into biblical texts once we shift our basic imagery from the monarchial God to the vulnerable God. Responsibility arises not only out of cause-effect relations; it also arises out of participatory relations. As parents have a share of responsibility in the actions of their children because they are so deeply involved with them, so the God of biblical faith, who is heavily involved in the life of a people, has a share of responsibility.

Those early stories in Genesis, the Cain-Abel one in particular, not only witness to our struggle with evil, but to God's pathos-filled involvement with our struggles. There is little in these stories that suggests that God foresees or plans the movements of events and the evils thereof; there is much to suggest that God is with us before our decision making and with us through the consequences, whatever they may be. The words that God addressed to Cain, "do well, purpose good, sin crouches at the door," could equally well be addressed to Eve when she is tempted by the serpent, to Sarah when she feels envy of Hagar's pregnancy, to Saul when he grew jealous of David's popularity, to David when he first glimpsed the married Bathsheba, to Judas when Jesus disappointed him, to Pilate when the crowd shouted for Jesus' life.

The God in these stories is one who is involved with us and responds to us, who calls us to decisions which often we fail to make. Sometimes that failure not only tragically breaks other people's lives but ours as well. Witness Cain's and Judas's.

But the tragedies that our decisions bring upon us and others extend to the eternal. There is a tragic element in the divine life—tragic because not even the sheer goodness of God can avoid a share of the responsibility for the evil that cuts into and across all our lives. What the Cain and Abel story has to tell us is not that God willed, planned, allowed, foreknew, and caused Cain to murder Abel, but that God is involved with Cain and Abel in their struggles to work and worship and to do good and avoid evil. That very involvement, which is a sign of God's love for us, ironically, tragically, brings upon God partial responsibility for some of the evils we inflict upon each other. It is ironic because God means goodness. It is tragic because God, who cannot abide evil, who opposes evil in all its forms, cannot draw us to greater and greater good without opening to us the possibility for greater and greater evil. That is the special anguish of the vulnerable God who is the Creator of the universe.

Yet that anguish of God, like the anguish voiced in Hosea and Jeremiah, like the anguish of Christ hanging on the cross, is good news. It is not the sign of a lesser love but of a greater love that God, in creating a world whose end is a kingdom of love and goodness, can only be that Creator through the anguish of sharing in the responsibility for the world's evil and suffering. The answer to Camus, if there is to be any answer at all, will not lie in denying a tragic element in either Christ—or God—as if Christ—or God—need to be protected from tragic pain. The answer lies in the felt insight that God's and Christ's tragic involvement in the world's evil is grounded in the love of God. God so loved the world even unto suffering with it and because of it. Yet that suffering has healing power in creating a community of love and forgiveness which lives to overcome the evil in the world.

The answer to Job and to Camus is also the answer to Baker. We can see now that the death of his father broke Baker's ability to worship a monarchial God. When the five-year-old Baker asks, "If God loves me, why did he make my father die," he is presupposing the monarchial image of God. When the adult Baker tells us that he "never cried again with any real conviction, nor expected much of anyone's God except indifference," he is expressing a refusal to worship a divine reality whose source of inspiration lies in sheer power. We can begin to answer Baker when we affirm him in this refusal. The Bible's evaluation of Job's words, "he has spoken of me (God) what is right," must be our evaluation of Baker's words. Baker cannot worship God conceived under the image of monarchy. He knows that God as the enemy, the one who crushes him. We must encourage Baker and those like him to let go of that image of God. We continue our answer to Baker when we clarify the source of our inspiration to worship God. It lies not in sheer power but in the vulnerability of God's love, a vulnerability which not only makes divine suffering unavoidable but, more significantly, allows that suffering to communicate God's love for us.

There is more to be said, of course. The discussion thus far points us to the farthermost boundary of divine vulnerability, that

horizon where the cross of Christ appears. The cross finally breaks
our old monarchial image of God and provides us with a new image.
In the crucified God, the christological God, we find the image of
vulnerability, the image of a God who redeems us not by coercive
power but by suffering with us in our suffering.

But there is a question prior to the christological one. The
monarchial image of God has firmly established itself in our minds
as a coherent, perhaps *the* coherent, conception of God. The
godness of God, so to speak, seems to lie in the very properties
that we associate with the monarchial image: controlling power,
foreknowledge, unlimitedness, independence, immutability, etc.
Even if we discover a biblical basis for a vulnerable image of God,
there is still the question whether the properties associated with
vulnerability, especially the property of limitedness, can be
conceived in terms of divine reality.

To that question we now turn.

4

God: Boundless
Yet Limited

A friend of mine, a middle-aged woman who has been a nun
for thirty years, said to me recently that she hardly dares any longer
to voice her thoughts about God to others. The problem was not
that God has become less important in her life. Quite the contrary.
It was more that her sense of God which developed over the course
of her life jars against her doctrinal understanding of God. Yet she
has no other way of understanding God than through these
inherited doctrines which now seem inadequate. The problem is
particularly acute in relation to her encounter with human
suffering. She no longer accepts the idea that such suffering comes
from the hand of God. That it is allowed by God stops her thoughts
when she tries in some coherent way to think out who God is.

As I listened to her I thought of those remarkable words in a
sermon broadcast in Spanish some days after the Mexico City
earthquake in September 1985. The priest was speaking to his
congregation from the steps of the church; the building itself lay
behind him in ruins. He said, repeating his words for emphasis,
"This earthquake was not sent by God. It came from natural forces.
It did not come from God." In the back of my head, like a distorted
echo, I heard Paneloux's words in Camus's novel *The Plague:* "My

children, this plague is a scourge of God, brought about by your lack of faith.''

Both the American nun and the Mexican priest have their theological roots in the same tradition represented in Paneloux's sermons. But something has happened to the religious consciousness in the decades that have passed since Camus wrote his novel. It would be misleading to suggest that the change lies in the reconception of God. The Mexican priest is no more likely to have a new or revised concept of God than my American friend. What is new is their experience of evil, and this has altered the way they interpret events which cause suffering. And they are not alone in this change of perspective.

We need to account for this change in the way we experience evil. Why do so many of us bridle at the thought of giving a positive religious significance to the destruction wrought by famine, flood and earthquakes, on the one hand, and by social poverty, war, and political tyranny on the other?

Many theories have been advanced to account for this change—from the increasing secularization of modern life to the development of a nuclear consciousness. But it is the media explosion, the presence of the camera in every remote corner of our life and our world, which has turned all of us into witnesses to evil like Rieux and Paneloux. We do not have to wait for the plague to come to our town in order to witness the random and senseless occurrence of pain. Pain appears in our living room every evening from 6:00 to 7:00 P.M. We merely need to flick a switch to see the grief-stricken face of some man, woman, or child suffering through some kind of human-made or natural catastrophe. This daily exposure to pain and despair in human lives destroys our easy religious answers. Most of us cannot bite Paneloux's bullet that these human horrors belong to the mystery of God's goodness. Instead, we simply watch as the experience of meaning drops out of large areas of human life.

Our problem is loss of meaning; it is not loss of understanding. In many ways we have never understood better the causes of destructive events. We know about the weather conditions that produce hurricanes and tornados, the geological conditions that produce earthquakes, the statistical probability of automobile accidents, the social conditions that cause riots and civil war, the ecological imbalance that poisons our air and waterways, the socio-psychological forces that can turn a civilized nation into a nation of fanatics, and so forth. But this kind of understanding does not provide us with the knowledge of meaning; it does not tell us what the purpose of these events are. After the earthquake in Mexico City in 1985, meteorologists appeared on the nightly news. They used three-dimensional models and computer simulations to help explain to us the instability of the Pacific coast undersurface. They talked about the shifting plates of the earth's crust, how these plates were wedged against each other, how the pressure would build, until finally, the plates, buckling under the strain, would slip and lurch. What they did not explain, and what wo do not know, is what positive meaning there is in the Mexico City earthquake or, for that matter, what meaning there was in the last Nicaraguan earthquake or what meaning there will be in the predicted California earthquake. To many of us, it all looks like random and purposeless wreckage.

On the one hand, we experience these events as senseless waste. On the other hand, we have inherited a theological tradition which sees God's good purpose behind all events. We live with this tension, this incoherence, between experience and doctrine. When the tension breaks, we do not necessarily experience loss of faith. We may, as my friend did, experience conceptual loss. My friend still confesses a faith in God. In fact, she believes that her faith is deeper and more mature than the one she professed as a twenty-three-year-old novice who saw divine purposes everywhere. What she has lost is a conceptual language for God—language that would allow her to talk about how God's power is related to forces of evil and destruction, language that would allow her to speak about what we can expect in terms of the fulfillment of God's purposes for the human race and, indeed, the whole creation.

Yet there is nothing new or odd about the fact that religious people may live without answers to these kinds of questions. We saw this phenomenon in our analysis of the faith struggles of Alyosha, Paneloux, and C. S. Lewis. The difference is that these three lived without answers to questions of the meaning of a particular set of events. They did not live without the assumption that God's good intent lies behind all events. They may have been pained and baffled by certain events, but they continued to believe that those events carried divine meaning, even though the meaning itself may lie beyond their comprehension. My friend's experience of evil placed her faith beyond the point of being able to assume divine intent or meaning in events that struck her as so much waste and wreckage.

My friend, though, did not respond as Ivan. She did not "return God the ticket." Nor did she deny God's existence. Of course, it is impossible in such matters to say with any certainty why people decide things the way they do. People feel the weight of opposing arguments, beliefs, and experiences in different ways. These weights are not objectively given. Most of the time it is not until we are in the midst of our struggle to come to a decision that we discover what feeling or idea weighs more for us, what experience counts more, etc. What continued to count for my friend was that God existed and was worthy of worship. What lost out in the mix of arguments, experiences, and beliefs was a set of interlocking notions of God which earlier I summarized under the image of God as absolute monarch.

Some years ago, I gave a public talk on the monarchial and vulnerable images of God in the Bible. I pointed to several places in the Bible where the vulnerable image of God seemed to be edging out the monarchial. The intent of the talk was to provide an alternative image to monarchy, but a good number of people wanted to affirm both images. A scientist who heard the talk rewrote the conclusion and sent me a copy. He was quite open to the notion of a vulnerable God, but he argued that the kingship of God must not be compromised. He therefore affirmed both the vulnerable and monarchial images of God, and held that their apparent contradiction contributed to the tension of a living faith. Perhaps this scientist was thinking that just as light sometimes behaves as if it were a wave and other times as if it were a particle, so the vulnerable image might sometimes seem to reflect the whole of deity and other times the monarchial image might seem to do so. As we cannot reconcile waves to particles, so we cannot reconcile monarchy to vulnerability. A living religion, like a living science, would use whichever image appears appropriate to the context.

This argument is very much like Barth's in his discussion of Nothingness. You will recall that Barth takes account of the modern experience of evil as senseless by locating evil not in God's will but in God's anti-will. Barth dissociates God from evil by implying that there are uncontrollable limits on God's will and power. At the same time, Barth's explicit thought continues to affirm that God has no limits. Barth saves the monarchial image in the same way that the scientist who heard my talk saves it: he tolerates an inherent contradiction, an element of incoherence, in his thought about God. Better incoherence, Barth seems to be saying, and apparently many of us join him here, than a denial of a concept or image as fundamental to our faith as an unlimited or monarchial God.

Still, incoherence normally serves as an impetus, or at least an openness to a creative change in our understanding. Scientists, for example, continue to look for a unitary theory of light that will account for its sometime particle, sometime wave, behavior. Barth's willingness to tolerate conceptual incoherence certainly cannot be attributed to his lack of creative ability. The answer lies more in the way that the idea of unlimitedness has fused itself to the reality of God. We can see how powerful this fusion is for us when we consider the case of a popular theology book which violated it.

When Harold Kushner's *When Bad Things Happen to Good People* was published in 1981, it offered religious counsel to people who suffered from personal affliction: illness, divorce, death of a loved one, etc. Books with such a purpose regularly come forth from the press. Yet the response to this one was remarkable in two related ways. First, nearly half a million hardcover copies were sold and the paperback edition quickly climbed over the million mark. Second, the book occasioned a theological uproar, not so much in the scholarly journals as in the popular religious organs of the church and even in the secular press. There are several reasons behind the great popularity of the book but there was a very simple reason behind the theological uproar it occasioned. In a book that was being widely and appreciatively received by Christian and Jewish laypeople, the author was suggesting that while there are no limits to God's love, there are severe limits to God's power. In a now famous and oft-quoted sentence Kushner had written, "I can worship a God who hates suffering but cannot eliminate it, more easily than I can worship a God who chooses to make children suffer and die." (Harold Kushner, *When Bad Things Happen to Good People*, [New York: Schocken, 1981], p. 134.)

In October 1982, the *Los Angeles Times* ran a long article containing interviews with sympathizers and critics of Kushner in order to lay out the pros and cons of his thesis. One of the critics stated the basic issue by pointing out that "the idea of a weak, empathetic God, no matter how much he suffers, is rather pathetic and unworthy of worship." This sense of a God unworthy of worship as the fundamental critique of Kushner's book surfaced again in two newsletters that are polar opposites in the world of religious publication. The first is from a bi-monthly newsletter written by Martin Marty, a well known liberal historian of American religion. In the November 15, 1982, issue, Marty comments on the recent explosion of articles attempting to make religious sense of suffering. Though Marty himself seems to be sympathetic to Kushner, he quotes a Jewish philosopher's judgment that "the idea of a limited God is profoundly unsatisfying." Marty summarizes the basis for the judgment this way: "To the degree that (God) is limited, he is on the same footing as all creatures, and thus it is pointless to call God, God."

The second newsletter is *Prison Fellowship*, published by a Washington-based group founded by Chuck Colson, an aide to President Nixon during the Watergate era and now a born-again Christian evangelist. In the March 1983 issue, Colson responds to Kushner in a more barbed way than that of the theologians, but his critique is the same. Colson argues that a God who is not all-powerful is impotent. Such a God, he writes, "isn't dead . . . just sick and feeble."

Three aspects of the response to Kushner are striking. It is taking place in popular organs; it locates the issue not only in doctrine, but on the more basic level of worship (is this God worthy of worship?); and it suggests that the array of people offended by the idea of a limited God contains an unusual mix of bedfellows, from liberal philosophers of religion to evangelical conservatives.

Kushner, apparently, struck two deep but conflicting chords in our society. On one hand, using the language and insights of both psychological counseling and religion, he has articulated a felt need in our time to dissociate God's hand not only from the massive forms of historical and social evil, but also from the personal tragedies that afflict individuals and families. But when the great "Yes" to Kushner died down, the underlying "No" began to be heard. I am not talking about an academic "No." The "No" that was heard came out of the church—perhaps, even out of the culture. It seemed to come from a place in our being which hardly required argument. The placing of limits on God's power was sensed as compromising the very feeling of awe which inspires our worship. People were asking how a God who lacked the awesomeness of omnipotence could be worthy of worship. Kushner's book simultaneously met a felt need and violated a felt sense. In doing this, he accomplished what academic debate almost never does. He brought into the light of public awareness the mutually obstructive character of two givens in the religious consciousness: God's unlimitedness and the need to dissociate God from senseless forms of evil.

I use the word "given" to indicate an idea which is so basic to our way of thinking that its validity goes largely unquestioned and it ceases to come under critical examination. Givens to us are like water to a fish: we would not notice them unless they were called to our attention. These ideas are like software in a computer: they are presuppositions to our thinking so we use them as the basis for our thinking rather than subject them to our critical scrutiny. In geometry, axioms function that way; in our religious thinking, the notion that God is without limits has come to function that way. That is why we respond so quickly and negatively, on both the level of feeling and intellect, to the proposal of a limited God. The phrase itself, "limited God," strikes us at once as religiously offensive and logically contradictory.

We need, of course, to be open to the possibility that such a phrase strikes us that way because it really is religiously offensive and logically contradictory. But until the origin of a given or presupposition is critically examined, our assumption that it is the case would find us guilty of circular reasoning. "Limited God" may strike us as an offensive and contradictory expression because we have already presupposed the notion that God is unlimited. Plato, for example, did not have that presuppostion. His system of thought was such that its logic required a notion of a limited God.

But from the point of view of Christian faith, the key question concerns not Plato's presuppositions but the Bible's presuppositions. Barth, for example, treats the unlimitedness of God as a revelatory given. As such, it functions as any other kind of given. Its "truth" has become the way we interpret the Bible and our experience. Those experiences, or lines of thinking, or even biblical texts which tend to question it, are themselves thrown into question. Barth's doctrine of Nothingness may raise questions about the validity of the concept of divine unlimitedness, but these questions do not lead Barth to alter his concept of God. They are simply seen as evidence of the limited character of human judgment. Thus, though Barth shares the modern Christian experience of some forms of evil as sheer negation, sheer opposition to God's will and power, he does not allow that experience to count against the doctrine of an unlimited God. Human reason and experience, Barth has always argued, must not be allowed to judge revelation. They must, therefore, subject themselves to it rather than stand over it.

The doctrine of Nothingness may find its origin in Barth's experience of the evil of Nazism, but precisely because it is rooted in human experience it cannot qualify a notion of God which Barth believes is rooted in revelation—though apparently it can be added to it. Barth's refusal to allow his doctrine of Nothingness to break the given of divine unlimitedness results in conceptual incoherence. But his willingness to accept conceptual incoherence would be seen by him as neither a failure of nerve nor of creativity. Quite the contrary. It would be a sign to him of the triumph of faith over reason, his own and ours.

But is the issue before us the conflict of faith and reason? Perhaps Barth is allowing the faith-reason issue to cloak another, more basic issue: namely, what are the grounds for the authority we give to the concept of an unlimited God? Did it become a given because it was grounded in revelation, or do we treat it as revelation because it functions as a given in our thought?

There are no simple answers to these questions. Certainly the tradition has interpreted biblical revelation as pointing to a God without limits. But the tradition never imaged the Bible as a coal mine with many veins, some of which have been worked upon for ages, others of which we have barely touched. When we image the Bible in this pluralistic way and consider the specific texts that support this pluralistic image, two conclusions, startling to our ordinary ways of thinking about the Bible, immediately follow. First, we lose the sense that the Bible clearly witnesses to God as unlimited in all aspects of being. Second, the notion of divine unlimitedness appears as an historical, provisional, and partial interpretation of the scriptural witness to God's creative and redemptive power. There is more complexity and ambiguity in the biblical witness to God than the theological tradition has allowed. Our task is not to deny the Bible's complexity and ambiguity, but to understand how its complexity works to strengthen our faith rather than confuse it.

Perhaps the key lies in our looking not at the history of our ideas about the authority of the Bible, but at the way the Bible has actually functioned in relation to our religious ideas and actions. When we look at the history of the church, we see that the Bible is used not only as the authority for doctrine and action but as a critique of earlier church doctrine and action. We can see this dynamic in Luther's critique of Thomism, in Calvin's critique of Luther, in the sectarian critique of mainline Protestantism, etc. We can see this happening even more clearly on such social-ethical issues as slavery, political and economic systems, male-female relations, war and peace, etc. Though the church's initial (and quite long-standing) reaction to slavery was to hold that the Bible allowed it, the Bible eventually functioned to convince Christians that faith and slavery were incompatible. Similarly the Bible came to be

heard not as providing a basis for a monarchial political system but
as the critique of it. In our own time, the Bible is coming more and
more to be seen as standing in judgment against the earlier
"biblically" based arguments for excluding women from the
ordained ministry.

The Bible helps both to form the way we think and act and to
challenge our formed thoughts and actions. The Bible does not
leave our thoughts and actions alone because there is always more
in the Bible than we take out of it at any given time. But it is true for
yet another reason. We are in a two-way relation to the Bible. We
hear God's voice through it, but we also use it to support our ideas
and values. We are always in danger of interpreting the Bible so that
God or God's will becomes a partial projection of our ideas and
values, rather than their judge and transformer. For that reason,
our concepts and images of God, as well as our ethical values,
should never be thought of as final truths immune to later criticism.

Those of use who criticize the tradition for ignoring biblical
passages which suggest the presence of limits in God cannot, in
turn, ignore the fact that the idea of a God without limits has its own
biblical roots. Because of this, we appear to be in the odd position of
pitting the Bible against the Bible. It is odd, but it is only logically
odd, not theologically odd.

In the history of its faith, the church always hears different
voices in the Bible. It has to struggle to determine which of these
voices is God's voice now, for this time, for this issue. I have already
noted this kind of dynamic in relation to such cultural institutions as
slavery, monarchy and the male priesthood. Of course, my earlier
discussion on Job also depended on the same kind of dynamic,
"living" understanding of biblical authority. It is time to pick up the
issue left lingering in that discussion. I had argued that the tension
induced by the experience of evil in the history of Israel was leading
Israelite faith away from the dominant, monarchial image and
toward the image of the vulnerable God. We need now to account
for why the vulnerable image of God was so largely ignored in the
history of the church's thought.

Why was the church so adamant for nearly two thousand
years in its refusal to allow any qualification to its interpretation of

God as unlimited in all aspects of being? We get a clue to that adamancy when we open ourselves to the possibility that we may have projected upon God our own historical, social, and psychological conceptions of what is ideal and valuable. In so doing, we blinded ourselves to the vulnerable image of God that now seems to jump out from so many texts of the Bible.

Let us begin with the way history affects our language and understanding of God. We sometimes forget that the Christian faith never had a chance to develop its life of worship, theology, and ethics in the cultural and religious soil of its origin. Almost immediately, and primarily because of political developments outside its control, the church was thrust into the Hellenistic world of the Roman Empire. In order to survive, the church had to address itself to people formed by Hellenistic, not Jewish, culture and religion. The effects were far reaching. They range from the fact that Jesus' words were remembered only in their Greek translation (and not in the Aramaic that he spoke) to the fact that the dominant theologians of the early church were all educated in and formed by Hellenistic culture and philosophy.

There is nothing wrong or even odd about the influence of Hellenistic philosophy, particularly Platonic modes of thinking, upon the development of early church doctrine. The very nature of the church drives it to become a universal community. In principle, the church seeks to express its faith both to all cultures and through the structures and thought forms of all cultures. But to say that the early church was right to think out its faith through Hellenistic philosophic categories does not mean that these categories are the only way, or even the happiest way, to express our faith.

Today, we can see that in our religious and ethical thinking we have a double inheritance. On one hand, there is the Israelite understanding of God's relation to the world, expressed through biblical narrative and prophetic utterance. On the other hand, there is our Greek inheritance of philosophical analysis and abstract definition. It would be false to suggest that there is an absolute distinction between the two. Also, by the first century we can detect the influence of Greek thought upon Jewish teachings. Still, there

are some very significant differences in emphasis. Greek philosophy from its beginning worked out its understanding of deity against
the backdrop of the anthropomorphic images of God presented in
popular Greek mythology. Philosophers thought of these myths as
providing an utterly false picture of God. God was considered as
beyond the kind of sufferings, bargaining, limitations, etc., that
were exhibited by the gods in these mythical stories. The history
of Greek philosophy exhibits an ever-intensifying tendency to
distance God from the limits of creaturely existence.

The Bible, of course, rejects polytheism. But it does not
hesitate to use anthropomorphic language and images to convey a
picture of God as outraged by injustice, repentant of past decisions,
sensitive to those who suffer, pained by disobedience, and so forth.
These kinds of divine limits, which are implied throughout the
biblical narrative, did not prove offensive to the mind and spirit of
ancient Israel, nor were they considered signs of God's imperfection. But to those early church theologians who came to biblical
faith out of late Hellenistic culture with its neo-Platonic assumptions of God's absolute transcendence, the notion of limits of any
sort was considered both offensive and a mark of imperfection.

Jürgen Moltmann, the German theologian, has recently
called our attention to the Greek virtue of "apatheia" as indicative
of the kind of metaphysical-ethical assumptions that the church
would have encountered in the Hellenistic world. (Jürgen
Moltmann, *The Crucified God*, [New York: Harper and Row,
1973], pp. 267–70.) Moltmann argues that Christianity's understanding of the perfection of God was affected by its acceptance
of "apatheia" as a virtue.

Apatheia literally means absence of feeling. This sounds like
an odd virtue to us because it suggests insensitivity to others. But in
the Hellenistic world it would signify freedom and independence.
The reason for this goes back to the way that Plato, and then the
neo-Platonists, associated change with appearance and not reality.
The argument goes this way: everything in this temporal world
changes and dies; therefore, everything that changes dies. On the
other hand, what is eternal is immutable. What is immutable must
be perfect. What is perfect must be complete. Change, then, of any

sort, even a change of feeling, would be a sign of deficiency or imperfection of being. To feel, to suffer, to be impassioned, are the marks of mortality and imperfection. Thus, lack of feeling becomes a virtue, and the "apatheia" of God becomes the cardinal sign of deity. God alone is free from the feelings, passions, and restlessness which relentlessly drive the rest of us.

Of course, the theologians of the early church knew well that the God of their faith was not inactive or indifferent to the happenings of the world. They clearly grasped the heart of biblical revelation as God's redemptive love for the world. But their Hellenistic heritage encouraged them to work out a doctrine of divine activity and love within the framework of "apatheia." They felt the need to reconcile the God witnessed to in Scripture with a Hellenistic culture's definition of perfection.

The brilliant resolution to this dilemma was to conceive God as unlimited in every aspect of being. The Greek perfection of fullness and completeness of being was translated into unlimited power, will, and knowledge. God is free and independent because there is no existing reality that can limit (that is, affect) God. This does not mean that God does not act upon and know the world in all its particulars, but that God's action and knowledge are part of God's eternity. They are there, so to speak, before the beginning of (the world's) time; therefore, they cannot be thought of as affected by the world's temporal actions.

We can see now that the tradition's desire to deny change, passions, and even openness in God was related to the Hellenistic virtue of "apatheia." That cultural idea, projected upon the deity witnessed to in Scripture, contributed to the hardening assumption that no limit whatsoever could be placed upon God's nature. Still, we must remember, as the church in our own time returns to the issue of divine limits, that the Bible knows very little about the Greek perfection of "apatheia."

It is not simply our cultural ideas or values that we project upon God's reality. As we examine the relation between God and the concept of unlimitedness, we need also to look at the way our political structures and social interests have entangled themselves with our thinking about God.

The modern discipline of sociology with its concern for the social origin of beliefs and attitudes alerted theologians to the political and economic dimension of religious doctrine. Of course, it is easier to see the way religious doctrines are sometimes used to promote social interests when we are talking about some other group's doctrine or a religion other than our own. For example, most of us can see that the white South African church's justification of apartheid is rooted not in revelation but in the political and economic interests of the ruling minority. In fact, some years ago, the World Alliance of Reformed Churches, a group to which the South African Reformed churches belong, declared apartheid a heresy. Not surprisingly, that judgment was rejected by the white South African Reformed churches.

In our own history, we can see now that those ante-bellum churches which appealed to the Bible to justify the institution of slavery were in part allowing their social interests to inform their interpretation of the Bible. The relative "purity" of the northern churches on this issue was in part due to the sociological fact that the institution of slavery was not tied heavily into the economic interests of the North. Similarly, those old theological arguments supportive of the divine right of kings, the subordinate role of women, the crusades, the inquisitions, have a strong, though hidden, element of economic self-interest in their sociological background.

It is easy enough then, for us to see that our economic self-interest can affect our use of the Bible on social issues. It is more difficult to see the connection between the notion of an unlimited God and our economic or political self-interest.

We can thank feminist theologians for noting one of those connections. They have suggested that there is a relation between the belief in God having no limits placed on "His" activity and the patriarchal sociological situation that prevailed throughout the church's history. In a patriarchal society, overt political and economic power is given to the male, considered by nature to be the dominant and aggressive sex. The woman, on the other hand, is thought of as naturally passive and receptive. She is accorded a subordinate and supportive role in society consonant with her nature. This sociological situation which distributes legal, psychological, and political power simply on the basis of sexual differentiation reflects, of course, the interests of the male. Traditional theology has interpreted the cultural differentiation in the male and female roles as ordained by God. It has also allowed its thinking about God to be informed by this cultural differentiation.

When we look at the properties that the tradition associates with God—sheer activity, initiative, unilateral and controlling power, impassibility, immutability, etc.—we see properties that a patriarchal society would identify as masculine. When we look at the properties that the tradition has denied in God—mutuality, openness to change, being affected by another, suffering, receptivity, passivity, etc.—we see properties that a patriarchal society would identify as feminine. In principle, we know that God transcends sexuality, and that males and females alike are created in the image of God. Yet, in fact, in our patriarchal society we use predominantly male images to refer to God, and we project upon God the values of the ideal male in their unlimited form. For example, it is not simply that God acts upon the world, but that God is pure act; there is no passivity in God at all. It is not simply that God has controlling power, but that God has unlimited power to control; there is no state of affairs that God cannot unilaterally alter. It is not simply that God's will has integrity of purpose, but that there are no constraints on the divine will. God could will anything (though God freely chooses only to will the good) and whatever God wills is enacted.

This analysis leads us back to the monarchial image of God. Only this time we are seeing it through the eyes of the feminist critique of a patriarchal culture. We know that in Western cultural history, the male has had the dominant leadership role, the female, the supportive, secondary role. What may not be so obvious is our tendency to consider the values associated with maleness as primary values, and therefore, the ones that would be appropriate to assign to God. It is no wonder that we become offended when values which we associate with a secondary, supportive role are attributed to God. There is something of Chuck Colson in all of us. We too may feel that a God who cannot act unilaterally and cannot right

wrongs with a word is "sick and feeble." Those other values which
we associate with the vulnerable image—mutuality, limits, anguish,
patience—do they not sound to ears long trained in patriarchy as,
shall I say it, "womanly"?

The issue is not so much whether the tradition compromised
the integrity of its redemptive faith in according such high value to
male experience. If we are to speak about God at all, we need to use
the language, images, and experiences of our society. We do not
think without metaphor, and we take our metaphors from social
experience.

It is not impossible, but it is extremely difficult for a people
to transcend their own cultural experience of what is of primary
value and what is secondary. The issue, however, is not what the
church did in the past, but how we are to respond today,
theologically, to our changing understanding of the roles of men
and women and the values associated with being male and female.

We are beginning to see today that any absolute separation
between the values we assign to males and females hurts rather than
enhances the full development of men and women. Both men and
women are active and receptive. The old separation between
primary and secondary values is surely a false one. Activity
(affecting others) is not superior to receptivity (being affected by
others), but the two are in a relation of mutuality. To be affected by
others means, of course, to be limited by others. And now we must
face a question difficult to answer because the weight of centuries of
tradition is in our head. Are we, in part, offended by the notion of a
limited God because of the undue weight we place on the culturally
conceived masculine properties of control and domination?

Let us now look at a psychological factor that lies at the root
of our offense at the notion of divine limitation. Kierkegaard first
provided us with a detailed psychological analysis of human
anxiety. He showed us the many ways we mask from ourselves the
anxieties that arise out of the inherent limits of our human nature.
Kierkegaard took our existential dread of death and meaninglessness and moved it to the center of our consciousness. He reminded
us that we cannot provide ourselves, or another, any surety whatsoever that we will live into the next second of existence. Nor can

we have any objective certainty regarding the meaning of our lives or the meaning of life as a whole. When we force ourselves to acknowledge the perils of existence and the uncertainties of our values, the anxieties of life overwhelm us and we fall into despair: a sense of hopelessness which is a sickness unto death.

Kierkegaard argued that faith alone, specifically faith in a God of unlimited, controlling power, can save us from the living death of despair. It needs to be faith, he said, because there are no objectively certain grounds for belief. Without the belief that history is under the divine control of a loving God, life is ultimately meaningless. But the arguments for this belief are no stronger than the arguments for disbelief. In fact, Kierkegaard went so far as to suggest that arguments for God hinder belief because they lead to self-deception. Neither arguments nor the living examples of the faith of others, but only the naked facing of despair will drive a person to make what Kierkegaard thinks of as the desperate leap into faith.

The late nineteenth and early twentieth centuries put a new twist on Kierkegaard's psychological analysis. Thinkers as diverse as the philosopher Nietzsche and the psychoanalyst Freud saw the leap of faith not as a lonely act of courage but as a failure of nerve. Nietzsche saw the loving, controlling God of faith as a God for the weak-minded who cannot tolerate the wild vitalities of life. Freud saw the all-powerful God as the projection of our own father upon the heavens. God was nothing more than the psychological coping mechanism thrown up by our need for affirmation and security in a world which is hostile or indifferent to our welfare.

Kierkegaard, Nietzsche, and Freud differ in their attitudes toward religion. But they all connect the concept of divine unlimitedness to the insecurity engendered by our own limits. For Kierkegaard, the conscious realization of our limits with respect to knowledge and power leads directly to despair, the sickness unto death. Only an unlimited God has the necessary resources to heal our despair. For Nietzsche, the sense of limits drives the weak to create a God who controls them, and drives the strong to an ever-widening breaking of limits—even though that breaking may lead to madness. For Freud, the overwhelming power of natural forces, the unknowns of existence, the ever-present threat of death, engender the psychic creation of a Father-God of unlimited power whose controlling, beneficent hand lies behind all events.

There are then powerful, psychological needs that are being met by a God of unlimited power and knowledge. In itself, this fact neither falsifies nor authenticates the concept of divine unlimitedness. It does account, though, for the strength of the psychological dimension in our "profound dissatisfaction with a limited God." If the psyche feels it cannot cope without a God of unlimited power, then it will fight hard to preserve its belief in that reality. Of course, we can argue that this presents no problem to theology. If our welfare requires that these psychological needs be met, that seems to support the argument that a redeemer God must be unlimited in power and knowledge.

We could say, for example, that when we call God Redeemer, we mean that God has the power to meet our needs in every dimension, including the psychological. Tillich used to remind us that when we project our ideas upon the cosmos, we are projecting them upon some reality—in the same way that a movie camera projects film upon a screen. The issue that Kierkegaard, Nietzsche, and Freud raise for us concerns not the reality of God but the ideas we project upon the divine reality. Do these ideas, rooted in our psychologically perceived needs, work for our fulfillment or to our detriment?

We find help in answering that question in a story written by the Czech novelist Milan Kundera in *The Book of Laughter and Forgetting* (New York: Penguin Books, 1981). The story is about an unhappy woman who was taken to an island where only children dwell. The situation on the island is Eden-like: all needs are provided for and the only activity is play. But there is no way to leave this paradise. The woman attempts to escape, she fails, and the children kill her out of revenge for rejecting them.

In an afterword to the book, Kundera says that he used children to portray paradise because of our tendency to lyricize and romanticize our childhood. But mature adults, marked by "memory and irony," find that a world composed only of children becomes a horror from whch they must escape. So it is, Kundera says, with all our dreams of paradise, our "age old dreams of a world where everybody would live in harmony united by a single common will and faith." Were our dreams to be realized, there would inevitably be some people who would stand in the way of the general harmony and the common will. "And so the rulers of paradise must build a little gulag on the side of Eden. In the course of time this gulag gets ever bigger while the adjoining paradise gets ever smaller."

Kundera, of course, is speaking about modern totalitarianism. His point is that "totalitarianism is not only hell, but also the dream of paradise." Communism begins with Marx's utopian vision; it is a vision of a world where there are harmonious answers to all the conflicts of life. But if these answers are to be actualized, total power must be given to the one who would enact them.

This analysis throws a startling light on our psychological need for a God of unlimited power and knowledge. We think that such a God has the power to fulfill our needs for harmony, security, and answers. But when we give total power to one reality, even to a loving reality, we do not clear the way to paradise. Quite the opposite is the case. Kundera's insight into the vision of a paradisaical harmony reminds us of the myth of Lucifer's fall. Lucifer was the "brightest" of all the angels, and yet he fell into conflict with God's perfect order. Even a highest angel "may stand in the way of the general harmony." The problem with projecting upon God unlimited powers to fulfill our psychological needs is analogous to the problem that arises out of our secular, paradisaical dreams. In both cases we give up human freedom. The problem is not that the loss of freedom is too high a price to pay for paradise. Rather, reality is such that it does not lie within our power to give up freedom. We are not free not to be free. The irony of our situation is that only a God conceived with limits can lead us toward a "paradise" appropriate for free beings.

Part of our difficulty with the question of limits may stem from our tendency to rely heavily on political imagery in our thinking about God. We want to think of God as highly as possible and we want to think of God as a person. We use imagery from family life to convey the loving, personal dimension in our experience of God. But to convey God's power we turn, understandably enough, to our political experience for an appropriate metaphor. There we find the absolute king, the ruler who aspires to total, unlimited power, and we apply this image to God—hoping, or assuming, that the dark side of totalitarian power would not contaminate the image. The failure of the tradition to resolve the problem of evil suggests that this was a faulty assumption. There is a darkness that clings to the notion of unlimited power. When we attach that notion to God we do not get rid of its darkness.

We need a metaphor other than that of the absolute monarch to convey the endless resources of God's creative and redemptive powers. That metaphor must image the dynamic and universal extensiveness of God's power without any suggestion of the totalitarianism that haunts the notion of unlimitedness. Neither the figure of the constitutional monarch nor of the president is adequate because both stand under the law rather than being the ground of the law. Perhaps we must go further afield than the worlds of politics and economics to find a new metaphor for God's creative powers.

We can liken God's power to that of the dynamic, ever-expanding character of our universe. We know now that we need to think "spherically," so to speak, about our universe. We know that in our curved universe all lines that radiate outward—in spite of appearing straight—will eventually approach each other and run together. We also know that as our universe curves out upon itself, it creates space rather than expands into space. In this sense, the universe is boundless: there is no such thing as a final, fixed boundary to the universe, nor is there any space bordering the outer limits of the universe. And yet the universe at any given time is limited in its extensiveness.

If we allow the universe to serve as a metaphor for the extensiveness of God's power, then we can think "spherically" about God. That will allow us to conceive of God as boundless yet limited—though, of course, in ordinary "flat world" thinking such a juxtaposition of terms would appear as a flat contradiction. As the universe is not in space but creates space, and is therefore boundless, so God's power is not simply in the universe but creates the universe and extends throughout it. As the universe is dynamic and yet, at any given time, has outer limits, so God's power is dynamic and yet limited. Thus does modern science, that human discipline which, in its own way, also seeks to understand the nature of the creation, provide us with a metaphor for a boundless, yet limited God.

Still, it is only a metaphor. We need to stop for a moment in our discussion to specify the ways in which God's power is boundless and the ways in which God is limited. The philosophical concepts of Alfred North Whitehead can help us here.

A Philosophical Interlude

In the 1920s and 1930s, Whitehead, a mathematician and physicist, wrote a series of philosophical books which in two ways went against the stream of the times. In an age when philosophers had given up the task of formulating a systematic understanding of the whole of reality, he developed a metaphysic which attempted to do just that. In an age when philosophy largely ignored or was critical of the concept of God, Whitehead's thought affirmed a divine reality.

Whitehead not only offended the philosophical establishment, he also offended the theological tradition. For although he maintained the necessity of a divine reality, he conceived of God as necessarily limited in certain aspects of being. Still, Whitehead's reconception of the notion of God and the world was like a liberating breath of fresh air for two groups of religious people: those who needed to reconcile the conflict between science and religion; and those who needed to reconcile the conflict between an all-powerful God and the enormity of the world's suffering.

Let us begin with an analysis of three basic Whiteheadian notions so we can gain a sense of his understanding of what it means to be an actual, living being.

To be is to be related to other beings. That is the first and perhaps most basic of all Whitehead's notions. Everything exists in a vast network of connectedness and interdependence. I cannot live without affecting others. I cannot live without others affecting me.

We can see this highly generalized notion exhibiting itself, without exception, everywhere in reality. All forms of life contribute to the life of others and depend upon others to contribute to their sustenance. Trees need water, soil, light, air, etc. The relative richness of the soil, the amount of water and light, the temperature of the air will affect the health and development of the tree. The trees themselves will help build up the soil and will provide protection and food for surrounding animal and plant life.

The brightness of the moon is but its reflection of the light waves thrown out by the vast fire of the sun. The heat in our bodies, and in all living bodies on earth, without which there can be no life, is but one of the ways in which we are related to and participate in those fiery events we call the sun. The movements of the earth, moon, and sun, the movements of all the planets and their moons, the movements of all the stars in our galaxy are each affected by and relative to each other.

We do not have our humanity without participating in a community of human beings. We learn speech and the arts and skills of life through relations to others. The values, purposes, and customs that we have depend, in large measure, on the kind of community to which we belong. I cannot begin to understand who I am unless I ask myself to whom I am related and to what community I belong. Nor can I understand other people and other things apart from knowing to whom they are related and to what community they belong.

The second basic Whiteheadian notion is creative process. To be is to become. It is to be caught up in a process or succession of connected becomings. At any given moment, every living actuality is driving itself to some new realization. Most of the time, the change is trivial, hardly noticeable. Other times, the change is momentous. Trivial or momentous, everything that is comes out of a past in which it was other than it is, and moves into a future in which it will become other than it is. This process is writ large in the evolutionary character of the development of forms of life on this planet. And it is writ small in each particular life, no matter how insignificant. The principle of creative drive is exemplified everywhere. Nothing is identical with what it had been the previous moment. The notion of sheer identity in time is a fiction.

I am not the identical person now that I was a moment ago, let alone a year ago, or ten years ago. Even as a minute passes, I breathe in some new air, perhaps carcinogenic air, which may eventually create cancerous cells running amok in my body. In that minute I might have felt someone's love or hate or anger or indifference. I might have gotten a new insight, entered into a new relationship, etc. In each moment, small changes, both physical and mental, take place in my being. They build upon each other, affecting the way I make new decisions so that over a long period of time things become possible for me that I might never have thought possible and I become the kind of person that I may never have thought I could become.

Whitehead's point is not so much that we have something happen to us. It is more that we continually create ourselves anew in the very process of experiencing and responding to our past and present worlds. We are touching here the source of freedom and its limits. All of us come out of a past and carry it with us in mind and body. Our past decisions, our past environment—including the immediate past—can lay the most severe limitations on what is possible for us. But Whitehead's argument is that it makes more sense to think of ourselves as making a determination out of the limits imposed upon us than to think of the past and present environmental influences making that decision for us. There is an element of self-determination—albeit sometimes a small one—in any living being's response to its world. God is among those influences affecting our decisions, representing for us the power to bring in a future which is more than the repetition of the past. Without God, only the past would be powerful. It is God who presents new aims to us, new possibilities for us, that free us from the otherwise totalitarian power of our past. In every moment of our existence God seeks to draw us into the kind of decisions which would lead us toward deeper and richer lives.

Whitehead's thought helps make sense of our moral and religious experience. There is a moral element in life because we make ourselves out of our past and, therefore, bear some responsibility for who we are and for the consequences of our acts. There is a religious dimension to all of life because it is God and not the past that sets before each living being a relevant aim for achievement. We cannot entirely reject God's aim: that would be to reject the order that makes our life possible. But we can modify the aim that God presents to us. God's relation to us does not and cannot abrogate the element of self-determination in our basic situation. God calls us toward our highest relevant possibility. But we always have other relevant possibilities of relative good and evil. Within those limits, we choose. Of course, sometimes the limits of relevance are so restrictive that all the possibilities before us involve pain and suffering to some degree. Illness is sometimes like that, divorce is usually like that, abortions are like that, being caught in the midst of a war is like that, and so forth.

We come now to the last of the basic notions: perpetual perishing. To be is to perish. It is the price paid for the creative drive to new life. If there is to be new being, the old must perish. What process leaves in its wake, so to speak, is the passage of events. Everything passes, no matter how good or beautiful an event was in the immediacy of its experience. The loveliness of summer does not last, no more than the summer of our lives. We are helpless before the perishing of things. Whitehead says that we "can't grab time by the scruff of its neck." This is the dark side of existence. It points to a tragic dimension which is present in all experience, even—perhaps I should simply say, also—experiences which participate most fully in joyousness.

Whitehead holds that what we do or feel is experienced by God; everything, in its own way, enters into the divine life. In this sense, our experiences and actions contribute to God's eternal life. But the intensity of my feeling for the beauty or joy of the moment passes; the intensity of *my* feeling of love for my child in a particular instant in my past is lost. God, Whitehead says, saves what can be saved. The everlastingness of God takes in each moment of temporal life as it passes. God feels my feeling and preserves it, but in that process there is a loss of immediacy. There is no avoiding the notion of limits even in a doctrine of salvation.

We have come upon the issue that cuts athwart the Whiteheadian and traditional understanding of God. The tradition has steadfastly refused to allow any element of limitation to enter into the doctrine of God. Thus, God is made an absolute exception to the notions or principles that help us to understand what it means to be something, or know something, or act upon something. We become something through relations to others, and we do not have our reality apart from a larger world than that of our own being. The tradition says that God needs no relations whatsoever and that the divine reality needs no world. We know some particular reality by experiencing it in its own time and space. I know my children because I have a history of experiences with them. I played with them, ate with them, worked with them, etc. In the thickness of time and the give and take of experience, I learn who they are, and they learn who I am. The tradition says that God knows everything at once in the simultaneity of eternity, in the instant of the eternal now. Finally, we act because we are acted upon by others and because there are others to act upon. The tradition says that God acts gratuitously, does not need others to act, and is unchanged by the temporal actions of others.

The problem of evil is only one, though perhaps the most important one, of the host of problems consequent upon making God an absolute exception to the limiting principles of being and knowing. Whitehead provides us with another way of conceiving the relation between God's being and our being. This way preserves the necessary distinction between God and the world, and yet avoids the negative consequences that inescapably adhere to the notion of sheer unlimitedness.

For Whitehead, God is the everlasting reason why there can be a world which exemplifies order, creative drive, goodness, and purpose. Of course, no particular world or universe is everlasting. Worlds have their beginning and their ending. Only God is eternal. Still, Whitehead asks us to reject the notion that God's reality can have meaning apart from a relation to some world. Instead we are to think of the goodness of God as lying in the perfection and universality of God's relation to the world. What does this change of view mean? What does it entail? It means, first, that we affirm

God's creating and redeeming activity in the world as the very essence of the divine reality. There is no real or essential God hiding behind these activities. God *is* Creator and Redeemer or, better still, God is everlastingly creating and redeeming. The traditional notion that the world adds nothing to God—that God's being, even apart from the world, is complete and perfect—can be arrived at only by an empty abstracting from God's creating/redeeming activity in the world. But God is not an abstraction. God is a living being acting upon and receiving from the particular activities of this world in this time.

This means that there is an aspect of God that is temporal, historical, relating, growing—that is, living. This is the aspect of God that knows events when they happen and responds to each particular event in a way appropriate to its highest possibilities and value for the whole. We do not have here the monarchial God who knows and controls our activities from eternity. There is some element of freedom in our responses. This means there is an element of risk in God's involvement in the world. Not everything is under control. Also, God is affected by our actions. What we do matters to God. God is vulnerable.

But God is also, everlastingly, the cause of our existence. There is an invulnerable, immutable, aspect of God—an aspect transcendent to the doings of the world. God may suffer from particular failures of response on our part, but these changes in God do not affect the goodness of God. No worldly act can affect God's power to create, redeem, know, forgive, love, judge, etc. God is and will be present with healing and transforming powers in the world, no matter what. God can never cease to be God.

In this sense, Whitehead affirms the tradition's insistence upon the independence of God. There can be no world without God, and God's reality cannot be threatened by the world. The tradition's error lay in assuming that if some aspect of deity is necessarily independent of the world, then the whole of deity must be conceived as necessarily independent of the world. Whitehead's contribution to Christian theology is a systematically developed view of God with two aspects or two poles. They can be distinguished from each other in nature and in function. But only in their interplay do we meet the whole of God's reality. Whitehead names these poles the primordial and the consequent.

When Whitehead says that God has a primordial nature, he is not talking about God having a beginning. He means that God is the beginning of the world—or, better, that the world begins in the vision of God. The envisioning power of God is the eternal basis for both God's creative activity and the world's. First, there must be vision. In the words of Genesis, God must first say, "Let there be light."

The primordial, then, is that aspect of God which transcends the world and goes before the world. Here God functions to provide the order which is presupposed by both the universe as a whole and the tiniest speck of existence. Everything that has life exhibits an order or structure which it requires in order to exist, but which it inherits rather than creates. We discover the presence of these orders in our study of astronomy, physics, chemistry, biology, and psychology. What we can never discover is why these interrelated orders persist into the next moment, though we know that if they did not persist, there could not be enduring life. God is not identified with any particular order. In principle, there could be a universe with a different order than the one we are members of. Perhaps there was one prior to ours. But God is the one who provides and maintains whatever order a universe exhibits; otherwise we would not have a universe but a chaos, "without form and void."

The creative act is not conceived here on the model of a watchmaker God who establishes a static order and then retires. Whitehead thinks of God's creativity in a dynamic way. Any given order contains within itself an element which in the past had disturbed some previously existing order; and this order is itself subject to disturbance from a new element. Order and novelty are not to be thought of as apart from each other but as interplaying elements in the creative adventure of the universe. God is the ground of any given order and, yet, God also provides the disturbing lure to novelty that seeks to advance that order toward increasing complexity and value.

Of course, God does not function simply as a general lure to the world. Whitehead conceives of God as providing specific aims for realization to every existing thing in each moment of existence. Each aim provided is consonant with our past but also seeks to lure us beyond mere repetition of the past. Whitehead's doctrine here seeks to account not only for the evolutionary character of our universe—the movement toward increasingly complex forms of being—but for the vivid sense of difference we all have, from time to time, between what we are and what we could be. God's presentation to us of realizable, though unrealized, aims is the source of our restless, zestful drive to creative achievement.

What are "aims"?

God's aims catch us between our desire for intense experience and our social or relational nature. We matter to ourselves (and therefore we want intense experiences), but our actions have consequences for others. God presents us with aims which balance our interests with the interests of others. In this way, God is the ground of our sense of value and wider meaning in life. God drives us toward an ever increasing consciousness of our being individuals belonging to a whole, where whole always includes some other whom we have left out. The mosquito seems content to live for the pleasure of the bite. God haunts us with ever-widening aims, so that we sense an emptiness in living for narrow purposes.

So far, I have talked about the primordial aspect of God, the aspect of God that preserves the tradition's sense of God's invulnerable and unlimited powers and knowledge. God alone has the power to provide order and drive to the universe. God's power here is boundless. There can be no state of affairs which can prevent God from exercising that power. God's knowledge of what is possible in this world or any world is also boundless. The capacity to see all possibilities is part of God's primordiality.

Whitehead points out that God as primordial is deficient in actuality. The power to provide an order is not the living act of providing a particular order. The knowledge of what is possible is not the living experience of some actual event or person. The knowledge of an ideal goal is not the same as experiencing even an approximate realization of that goal. When we are talking about *this* particular act of God, for example, God calling Moses to lead Israel out of Egypt, or this particular knowledge of God, for example, God knowing about David's order to have Uriah die in battle, we are talking not about the primordial but the consequent aspect of God.

The consequent refers to the temporal, relational, historical dimension of the divine reality. Here is the aspect of God that finds its exemplification in the dynamics of biblical narratives: the God who deals with the particular perversities and unpredictabilities of people and events; the God whose feelings run from anguish to joy to regret to hope; the God who knows our feelings as we experience them. Whitehead's doctrine is that God knows and feels things not only as they are known and felt by the world, but as they are qualified by God's own loving will and good intent for the world. God feels Jesus' anguish at Gethsemane, but God also fuses that feeling with the sense of a new community that can emerge from the cross of Christ. God feels the world's relative indifference in the early 1940s to the German roundup of European Jews. God also feels the Nazi's triumphant elation and the shocked pain of the Jew. God feels all this with a love which is vulnerable (is there any other kind of love?), and therefore hurts; with a love which is just, and therefore judges; with a love which is compassionate, and therefore ready to forgive. Here, forgiveness means ready to call us to bring some good out of the wreckage we have wrought.

In the consequent aspect of God, the world's life enters into God and is there given everlastingness. It is transformed by God's way of feeling the world. And it returns to the world in the form of particular aims to draw from us an increase of love and creativity.

We are talking here not only about God's vulnerability but God's becomingness. Every act in the world adds to God's being. Our actions have consequences not only for others but for God. The music of Mozart contributes not only to our lives but to the everlasting life of God. And so it is for us. We contribute to God's glory and we contribute to God's pain. In one way or another, our actions add to the richness of God's being or the depth of God's suffering.

The dimension of becomingness in God does not mean that God becomes something other than the loving, just Creator and Redeemer. It would be truer to suggest that the becomingness of God allows God to be God. God always feels and responds to the world in ways appropriate to God. The integrity of God is unalterable. God's becomingness means that the perishing that characterizes everything worldly is not the final word that is said to our lives. Our lives are saved from being mere passage, ultimately signifying nothing, precisely because the feelings and events which make up our lives enter meaningfully into God's life. Thus, it is the becomingness of God that saves that which in its nature cannot be saved. It is God's consequent nature which gives everlasting value to that which is finite and temporal.

When we talk about God feeling or experiencing the world, we are talking about the second mode of divine knowledge. There is another, prior mode of divine knowledge. As primordial, God eternally envisions or knows all possibilities. In this sense, nothing that actually happens takes God by surprise. In another sense, given the element of self-determination, what actually happens in time is a surprise. Also, the knowledge of the possible is not the same as the knowledge of the actual. It is, for example, one thing to know of the possibility of being a parent, and quite another to know what a parent is by being one. The same is true of love or leadership or failure or suffering. The book of Samuel suggests that Saul grasped eagerly for the possibility of kingship (1 Sam. 11:15). He knew as possibility what a king was. Perhaps he even knew, in theory, the risks. But the actuality of kingship gave him a new kind of knowledge, and made him the tragic failure of a figure that we find on the pages of the Bible.

God knows actual events through the consequent nature. God's knowledge of the actual is consequent to the occurrence of an event. Still, God's knowledge, even God's consequent knowledge, can be considered perfect knowledge. But perfection must be understood in its dynamic sense. God is in relation to all things as they achieve actualization. Therefore, God's knowledge is universal and immediate. This means that God knows every event as it occurs. Of course until an event actually occurs in some particular time and in some particular space that event is not there to be known. It is not a mark of imperfection not to know what cannot be known.

In the world of nature, the element of self-determination is relatively small. Accurate knowledge of some being's past behavior gives us the ability to predict its future behavior. But predictability is never absolute, and becomes less and less so as we move up the evolutionary scale toward human life. It is not simply because we are limited in our knowledge that we cannot predict our future behavior. Because we are free, we sometimes have the experience of being mysteries to ourselves. But also, because we are free, we are in a very particular sense a mystery to God. It is not only Saul, for example, who had to wait upon time and experience to discover what it meant for him to be a king. God also had to wait, though not in a passive manner. God is there in every moment of Saul's life seeking to draw from him decisions that might achieve a rich rather than a tragic life. Saul, like all of us, had to struggle not only with God but with the power of his past life and insecurities. Saul's freedom, like our freedom, does not render God's power passive. We have every reason to believe that God was working with Saul to draw from him decisions that would have made him a successful king. But the text does not suggest that God's power is coercive or controlling. Saul's struggle was a real struggle; its outcome was not there to be known, even by God, until it reached its tragic conclusion.

One final point about Whitehead's concept of God: God is *one* reality, primordial and consequent. When we encounter God, we encounter the whole God, not the primordial God "here" and the consequent God "there." In this respect, the two poles of God's being are analogous to the form and weight of a box. We never encounter simply the form of a box or the weight of a box. We encounter the box, formed and weighty. So it is with God. We do not sometimes encounter a God who has limits and other times a God without limits. We encounter the whole God with boundless resources to make the perfect response within the very real limits of our past and present environment. God can only do what is possible in a created universe which has had and continues to have its own historical "say" in the way things are. There are limits. But what is possible in any given situation far exceeds the limits of our vision— and God is boundless in the envisionment of what is possible.

God's boundless power to envision relevant possibilities, to preserve the achievements of the world, and to lure the world toward increasing creativity and love does not in itself resolve the problem of evil. But Whitehead's suggestion that we conceive of God as primordial and consequent helps faith make a sufficient dissociation between God and evil. Still, it is not in the doctrine of God that Christianity states its response to the problem of evil. Rather, Christian faith points to the life of Christ, and to that Christ-formed community, the church, as the place where evil is encountered and overcome.

5

The Christological
Vision of God

We need to talk about the power of suffering love. We have
come to the cross of Christ. Here is the starting point for the
Christian answer to the power of evil in our lives and in our world.
And yet it has taken more than a hundred pages to arrive here. We
could not speak about Christ until we first raised fundamental
questions about the image and understanding of God that we bring
into our lives under Christ. We needed to become alert to the
cultural sources of our ideas about God so that we can heed the
warning of the Japanese theologian Kitamori that "when we see
only the historical Jesus and not the pain of God, we have known
Christ after the flesh only." Perhaps Kitamori's phrasing is too
sharp. Still, it is well taken, for it reminds us that for centuries the
church had difficulty affirming God's suffering in the cross of
Christ. The church was too much ruled by the monarchial and
invulnerable image of God.

The theological tradition, of course, never hid the texts of
Christ's suffering from us. Quite the opposite. Images of Christ's
passion dominated the art and architecture of the church. We can
see now that the tradition helped us interpret those texts so that we
could avoid attributing suffering and vulnerability to God. In so

doing, it saved us from the shock and embarrassment of confronting the suffering of God. It is always shocking and embarrassing to face others in their suffering—especially when God is the subject of the suffering. Yet the way toward understanding the redemptive power of suffering love is through the shocking experience of God's suffering on the cross.

Paul says, "for I delivered to you, as of first importance what I also received, that Christ died for our sins " (1 Cor. 15:3). Paul does not begin his rehearsal of the Gospel with the sending of Christ—as in the fourth Gospel—or with the birth of the Christ Child—as in Matthew and Luke—or with the baptism—as in Mark—or with a teaching or healing or miracle of Jesus. He begins by stating the redemptive significance of Christ's death.

We need to remember that for Paul the words "Christ died" would be filled with shocking power. We hear those confessional words through a tradition that developed after Paul's death. For us the confession of Christ's suffering and death presupposes a redemptive interpretation of the suffering and the death. We understand Christ's death as the atoning price God paid for our sins, or as the means God chose to defeat death and the devil—depending on which of the two traditional theories of the atonement that we prefer to follow. But Paul, as a first-century Jew, did not have that "knowledge." He encountered the crucified Christ without the doctrinal interpretation of the later church. Even the gospel, since it was not yet in written form, could be known to him only through Christian preaching. And he would have heard that preaching through the mental filter of one who was the enemy and official persecutor of the church. When Paul encountered Christ on the road to Damascus, he did so with Jewish expectations of who the Christ was. His hopes were in a triumphant, not a crucified Christ.

There is a Hasidic story about a rabbinic student who was not able to pass down the teachings of his rabbi. This was because the rabbi would always open his commentary on a biblical text with the phrase, "God said" or "God spoke." The student would become overwhelmed by the thought that "God spoke." Each time he heard those words he would begin to bang his head and fists against

the desk repeating aloud, "God spoke, God spoke." He would
become so beside himself that his fellow students would have to
carry him out of the room.

We cannot, of course, get inside Paul's consciousness to
discover what he felt when first he heard the words, "Christ died."
But we can imagine that they were even more overwhelming to him
than were the words, "God spoke," to the rabbinic student. For a
first-century Jew, the Christ, the Messiah, was the one longed for,
the sign of God's coming kingdom, the one who would bring in the
new age of justice and peace, the one who would still forever
Israel's cry of anguish: "How long, O Lord, how long?" Israel had
pinned its faith and hopes on a Messiah coming with power to
destroy, once and for all, the enemies of God's righteousness. To a
heart and mind formed by this Jewish tradition, the church's
proclamation that "Christ died" would have been heard and felt
as blasphemy.

Earlier in his first letter to the Corinthians (1:20), Paul said
that the preaching of Christ crucified is folly to Greeks who seek
wisdom, and a stumbling block or scandal to Jews who seek signs.
Surely he was talking out of his personal experience as a Jew
seeking signs. Christ on the cross was not a messianic sign—quite
the reverse. As long as Paul looked for a Messiah with kingly
power—as the world understands kingly power—he could only be
repelled or scandalized by the salvific confession, "Christ died."
But what could break Paul's assumption that Christ comes with the
monarchial power of God behind him? The answer lies in the
Pauline affirmation that God was in Christ.

It is easy to miss the shift in Paul's understanding of Christ.
As long as the Christ is thought of as the "King of the Jews" sent by
God to lead Israel to victory over God's enemies, then it is
blasphemy to proclaim the suffering and death of Christ. From this
perspective, the suffering and death of Christ could only mean the
failure of God's plan of redemption. But Paul's understanding of
Christ and of God's mode of redemption has changed. The death
of Christ does not mark the end of redemptive hope, because *God*
is in Christ. It is God the eternal Creator who suffers in Christ's
suffering and death, and this is a very different matter from thinking

that the kingly agent sent by God has met his death. Christ's suffering can be redemptively powerful because it is the suffering of One who cannot be overcome or defeated by suffering. The redemptive power encountered in the life of Jesus can be encountered again and again in the life of the church. That redemptive power is the power of God's suffering love. The church knows that power in and through the life of Christ. The God we confess as our Creator and Redeemer is a suffering or a christological God, a vulnerable God, or, in Moltmann's dramatic phrase, "a crucified God."

In the earlier chapters, I indicated the church's historic resistance to the idea of God's suffering. I also made suggestions about some of the origins of that resistance in order to help us come to grips with our own resistance. But the discussion of Christ's suffering raises a point of resistance tied in with the church's apocalyptic hopes. These hopes can be stated this way: in the first coming, Christ comes as the vulnerable one, the one who suffers for us; but in the second coming, Christ will show himself as the monarchial Christ, the one who comes with coercive power. This way of distinguishing between the first and second coming hides the fear that God's suffering in Christ lacks real power. We think that real power is coercive power, the power of irresistible force. Two responses must be made to this fear.

The first concerns our tendency to equate power with the capacity to impose forcibly or violently our will upon the other. In Walker Percy's novel *The Second Coming*, the insolence of a waiter enrages Will Barrett, the central figure in the story. Barrett wants to pummel the waiter, and he barely manages to restrain his violent impulses. As the rage passes, he asks himself:

> Where does such rage come from? From the discovery that in the end the world yields only to violence, that only the violent bear it away, that short of violence all is in the end impotence? (Walker Percy, *The Second Coming*, [New York: Washington Square, 1980], p. 198.)

We do not have to look very far to find that place where we discover that "in the end the world yields only to violence." The history of nations and peoples is largely the history of wars and the forceful domination of one group over another. Every nation in the

Americas is ruled by the descendants of Europeans. If we ask ~~violence~~ ourselves "why?" the answer is that the English, the French, the Spanish, the Portuguese, and the Dutch who came to the Western hemisphere in the seventeenth century had a capacity to inflict violence far superior to that possessed by the native populations. In more recent times, it was Russian tanks that put an end to Hungary's attempt to work out a "socialism with a human face," and it was American marines that ended Marxist rule in tiny Grenada. In ancient times the Pax Romana was maintained only as long as Rome could field a military force superior to those peoples who lived within and across the borders of the empire. And, of course, there is a long list of peoples and cultures that disappeared because they were either annihilated by or absorbed into their more powerful and violent enemies.

The Bible is not unfamiliar with this "discovery that in the end the world yields only to violence." The apocalyptic vision in Mark 13 spares only the elect from the destructive power that God unleashes upon the creation. In the final battle envisioned in Revelation 20, the enemies of God are destroyed and Death and Hades are consumed by fire. Even the prophet Habbakuk, who was outraged by the "violence" he saw all around him, expressed the hope for a final violence, this time a divine one (3:4–16). There is a strand in our biblical inheritance which envisions redemptive existence as lying on the other side of a divinely wrought, cataclysmic event which destroys those opposing God's will. This biblical vision of a final violence is in our consciousness. It finds political expression in our talk about good and evil empires, and its literary expression can be seen in books as diverse as *The Late Great Planet Earth* and the "Hobbit" fantasies of the popular English writer Tolkien.

But there is in the Bible another vision, a vision which runs counter to the assumption that only violent power is ultimate power. It finds expression in Isaiah's vision of a lion and a lamb lying down next to each other. We can see it in Jesus' command to forgive sins endlessly, and in his teaching that "those who live by the sword will die by the sword." It is present in a text in the book of Hosea:

I will not execute my fierce anger, I will not again destroy Ephraim; For
I am God and not man, the Holy One in your midst, and I will not come
to destroy. (11:9)

Hosea's prophetic utterance suggests that violence is *our*
final solution but not God's. We may be tempted to think that "in
the end the world yields only to violence" but that may reflect not
the divine vision but the distortion and limitations of the human
vision of what is possible.

This counter-vision also finds a basis in human experience.
We know that violence breeds hatred and further violence. Abused
children are likely to become abusive parents. Parents whose
authority over their children depends on the regular use of physical
force do not see themselves as potent parents but as failing parents.
What we find in the family, we find also in our political experience.
In South Africa, the white minority's continued use of violence to
maintain its power and wealth can only lead to further violent
explosions of black majority wrath that work to the good of neither
black nor white. The list of peoples whose history of violence with
each other has led them into a present of hatred and murder is
legion: the Catholic and Protestant in Northern Ireland, the Arab
and Jew in Israel, the Turks and the Armenians, the Cambodians
and the Vietnamese, and so on. The "discovery that in the end the
world yields only to violence" runs into the counter-discovery that
violence leads to annihilation and not redemption or transformation. Violence, even divine violence, is not really a solution to the
problem of evil and suffering. At most, it destroys the evil-doer, but
it also denies forgiveness and the possibility of the redemptive
transformation of the evil one.

There is a second response that needs to be made to our fear
that the suffering love of God revealed on the cross lacks ultimate
power. Violence is related to unilateral, controlling power: the
ability of one being to violate the integrity of another by the
imposition of will. The religious vision of a violent end is fed by the
monarchial concept of God's controlling power and will. We are
back again to the fact that we allow monarchy to be the normative
image in our thinking about God. Only this time, since the biblical
image of the end is tied in with the second coming, the image of

monarchial power is informing our understanding of Christ. In principle, the church affirms the fullness of divine revelation in Christ. In principle, then, the life, death, and resurrection of Christ reshape our understanding of God's redemptive power. But instead, the redemptive action of Christ has been interpreted through the monarchial image of God's controlling, unilateral power. This is apparent not only in the apocalyptic interpretation of the second coming but also in the dominant interpretations of the atonement. Whether we are talking about Christ defeating demonic powers or Christ being a full propitiation for our sins, both doctrines of the atonement indicate a cosmological action or transaction that requires no action on our part. It is a unilateral act of a kingly God which requires no participation from his subjects. The most that is required of us is the faith that God has acted in Christ to redeem us. And, even here, heavy-handed interpretations of grace sometimes suggest that our faith is rooted not in our free will but in God's irresistible will.

The situation, then, is this. Just as the Bible contains strands with conflicting images of a monarchial and a vulnerable God, so the New Testament contains conflicting images of Christ's work. The issue is not which of those images is biblical—they all are biblical—but which do we allow to dominate our understanding of God and our lived faith? The New Testament pictures Christ as one who gives his life for those who have betrayed him, who forgives those who have killed him, who goes out in compassion to weak and corrupt tax collectors, who eats with sinners, and who is hard on righteous, religious people because he thinks they are tempted to be judgmental. This is a picture of a Christ who judges others, such as the woman caught in adultery or the Samaritan woman with many husbands, not in order to condemn or to destroy, but to transform. The New Testamant also pictures Christ as the judge-king on his throne, separating the sheep from the goats and casting the condemned into eternal torment, and as the conquering king in battle defeating, once and for all, the evil ones. In this picture, Christ's judgment leads neither to transformation nor to redemption of the judged ones but to their annihilation.

There is no simple answer to the question why the New

Testament contains conflicting and contrasting images of Christ's work. Ancient Israel, in the course of her thousand-year history, came many times to reunderstand the nature of her hope, and she developed a multiplicity of ways to picture God's mode of redemptive activity. The early church inherited this plurality of hopes and pictures. Perhaps the key to answering this question lies in Reinhold Niebuhr's insight that the Christ who came was not the Christ who was expected. Christ was expected to establish God's kingdom on earth. Instead, Christ went to the cross. It is understandable that as much as possible, the church would try to minimize the distance between expectation and realization. The church too needed signs; it searched the Hebrew Scriptures for texts that would affirm Christ as fulfilling expectations. By so doing, the church felt that it strengthened its claim to legitimacy. But there was a price to pay. The more the church saw Christ as fulfilling the expectations of Israel, the less it was scandalized by its proclamation that "Christ died." That Pauline sense of being shocked or jolted by God acting against our expectations and assumptions was lost. Thus the church lost the impetus to question or at least clarify traditional understandings and images about the nature of God's redemptive powers. It would be as if, after reading the book of Job, we returned to the comforters' arguments to account for Job's repentance.

Still, it would be too much to suggest that Job's critique and the cross of Christ had no affect on the dominance of the monarchial image of God in the life of Israel and in the church. Israel continued to think of God as having controlling power, but the book of Job was canonized. That meant that Scripture contained a book which critically called into question the tradition's basic assumption of the nature of God's power. Similarly, the cross is in the New Testment, like an unexploded bomb, sitting uneasily amid traditional interpretations which appear to defuse it by making it consonant with the monarchial image of God.

We need to let the cross explode the tradition's interpretation of Christ and God. Of course, when we say *the* tradition, we are talking about two thousand years of *our* tradition. It is difficult for us to think of the cross in contradiction to the traditional image of God. For that to happen, we need a shift of perspective so that we can see and sense the cross' shocking power. But how can we do that?

I do not know the answer. I am not sure that in matters of faith we can ever answer the question of how to shift a perspective. But we can point to places in the church and in the lives of individuals where this shift in perspective is occurring. I have already mentioned Moltmann and Kitamori as theologians who are seeking to redefine God's power in terms of pain, suffering, and defeat. Perhaps their rethinking was occasioned by the shock of experiencing the militaristic aggression of Germany and Japan in the late thirties and early forties, and then their crushing defeat in 1945. For a different kind of reason, third-world liberation theologians, who identify strongly with the poverty and suffering of their people, tend to see Christ's pain as God's pain, and to connect that pain to the long history of social oppression. But it would be a mistake to give the impression that the change of perspective that we are talking about is confined to professional theologians or is occasioned only by a radical political experience. Consider the following remarks, taken from a letter by a college student who had been brought up in the church. She had been reading about gnostic Christians, an early church group whose doctrines and written versions of the gospel were considered heretical by the orthodox Christian churches.

> I wanted to tell you about one neat thing the gnostic gospels suggest. The gnostics couldn't reconcile what they termed the Creator God, who was very vengeful (in the Old Testament) and the Christ, a God of mercy, love, and forgiveness (in the New Testament). The Creator God was different from the Savior God. The way I want to interpret it, however, is that Christ made possible the suffering character in God, that there actually is a changing character in God. But wait a minute: it's hard for me to believe that before Christ all these people had to deal with some horrible, vengeful God. I don't know. But I see Christ's crucifixion as transforming the nature of God, or at least making that nature manifest for the first time. I find this so interesting because until last year I said I believed in God, but I didn't know what to do with Christ; I didn't know if I "believed" in him or how to believe in him. Now my very faith rests on what Christ represented. I could not believe in God now if I didn't understand and believe in Christ. That is quite a drastic change.

The reference to gnostic Christianity helps remind us of a false, dualistic way to allow our encounter with Christ to affect our understanding of God. The gnostics saw clearly enough that in Christ something radically new had entered into God's way of relating to us. Their error was to interpret that newness in terms of Persian (Zoroastrian) cosmological dualism. They argued that we had been related to the Creator God of evil, but now, through Christ, we are related to the Savior God of goodness. For the gnostics, then, Christ did not transform our way of understanding our relation to God, but annihilated our faith in the God of our past. The church was certainly right in resisting the temptation to split off the God of Israel from the God of the new Christian community.

What interests me about the letter is the way it moves from finding Christ problematic to giving Christ the authority over our understanding and confessing of God. That shift is not made in a gnostic, dualistic fashion. Christ does not annihilate our faith in the God of our tradition but represents or re-presents that God to us so that our understanding of God is transformed. And it is that transformed understanding of God which allows the writer to "believe in God now."

We are not told what critical event or thoughts lay behind the letter writer's shift of perspective from God to the suffering Christ. But we cannot go far astray if we imagine that behind all our present-day theological struggles with the problem of evil and God's power lies the memory of Nazi Germay's cruel, systematic annihilation of millions of European Jews. Who among us has not seen pictures of the roundup of Jews and the unbearable horrors of the death camps? This "inhuman" abuse of power, these images of massive suffering by helpless people, are seared into our conscious and unconscious memory as a symbol for us of the power of evil, the ever-present "No" to God's never-ending "Yes."

Elie Wiesel, a survivor of the death camps, relates an incident in his novel *Night*, that dramatizes, oddly enough, the christological movement of faith in our time:

> The SS hung two Jewish men and a boy before the assembled inhabitants of the camp. The men died quickly but the death struggle of

the boy lasted half an hour. "Where is God? Where is he?" a man behind me asked. As the boy, after a long time was still in agony on the rope, I heard the man cry again, "Where is God now?" and I heard a voice within me answer, "Here he is—he is hanging here on this gallows."

This is a powerful story. Part of its power rests in its startling, concluding image—God hanging on the gallows. We are taken aback when we are unexpectedly confronted by it. Of course, the power of the story depends, in part, on our lack of expectation. We need to ask ourselves why, after two thousand years of Christianity, we are surprised by the image of God hanging on the gallows. We need also to ask ourselves how Wiesel could give that answer.

We can begin by noting Wiesel's opening question, "Where is God now?" Sometimes the very wording of a question places limits on the possible range of answers. Perhaps our questions regarding the problem of evil have been too limiting. We have tended to ask, "Why, God, are you doing this?" or "How can you allow this, God?" or, more academically, "How can God be all loving and all powerful when there is so much suffering and injustice in the world?"

Wiesel's question, "Where is God now?" is a less limiting question than those we are used to. Perhaps it is therefore a better question. It is not loaded with traditional, theistic assumptions of God's power and control over events. It is not a question which demands that God be able to justify this evil event. The question is so worded that it allows Wiesel to give—dare I say it—a christological answer.

I worry about suggesting that a practicing Jew is thinking christologically about God. Perhaps such a statement should not be made. It is too given to misunderstanding. I certainly do not mean that Wiesel is drawing on any other tradition than the Jewish tradition. By asking the less limiting question, "Where is God now?" Wiesel opens himself to that neglected biblical tradition of the vulnerable God, the God who identifies with the victim, and whose own suffering becomes the speech of love. From the Christian point of view this is a christological image. Of course, Wiesel must be aware of that. Perhaps, in an unconscious sort of way, he is even beholden to it. Still, from the Jewish point of view, it is the image of the God of pathos, present in both Hebrew Scriptures and in Jewish esoteric literature.

There is something more to be said on this point. The context of Wiesel's question and answer is an extraordinary one—a boy hanging on the gallows, weighing too little for the stranglehold of the rope around his neck to give him a quick death. In the discussion of Paneloux, Barth, Job, even Moltmann and Kitamori, we have noticed that the experience of intense suffering takes the monarchial image of God to the breaking point. But surely it is not simply the experience of suffering that moves us confessionally to the christological vision of a suffering, vulnerable God. We must also be able to sense, even if only dimly, the hidden presence of a suffering God amid the horror of human pain. There is revelation, grace, and mystery in the confession of the vulnerable God.

We are ready now to deal with Colson's charge that all our talk of divine suffering and pathos will lead us to a God who is "sick and feeble in relation to the power of evil." We can let Colson's questions become an occasion for our questions. How can God's suffering lead into a triumph over evil? How can I worship a God whose creation seems to have gotten out of divine control?

We can begin with the assumption that suffering is strictly a passive power and that the best it can promise us is divine sympathy. If nothing more could be said about the power of suffering, then it is clear enough that the experience of God's presence might help us endure suffering, but that the power of evil would be left undiminished, or even enhanced. But there are forms of suffering which are active as well as passive. We need to talk about the ways in which God's suffering brings a transforming element into a destructive event so that its power of evil is diminished and even overcome. It would be a mistake to interpret the shift from the monarchial, theistic image of God to the vulnerable, christological image as a bow to realism—as if the rampant injustices, unfairness, and cruelty in life finally force us to surrender our hope for "a new heaven and earth." When we give up hope in God's redemptive powers, we are not moving to a new image of God but to atheism. Let us talk then about christological powers, the powers that we associate with the passion of Christ: suffering love, vulnerability to others, limitedness. How can we understand these as active, redemptive powers of God?

I begin with the story of the Grand Inquisitor from Dostoevsky's *The Brothers Karamazov* (New York: Macmillan, 1923). It is a story within the story of the novel. It has been composed by Ivan who tells it to his Christ-like brother, Alyosha, as a way of expressing his own assessment of human life. The story is laid in Spain during the Inquisition. Christ returns, is recognized and hailed by the people, but is quickly arrested and brought to the cardinal, the Grand Inquisitor. The cardinal castigates his prisoner. He condemns Christ's teachings of freedom and love. Such teachings, the cardinal argues, are beyond the capacity of the masses of weak, cowardly, and vicious human beings. He calls Christ's mission a failure and sees the church's function is to "correct thy work." People must be controlled for their own good. Since a living Christ is a danger to the work and authority of the church, the cardinal condemns him to death: "tomorrow I shall burn thee." The story ends this way (Ivan is talking):

> "When the Inquisitor stopped speaking he waited some time for his Prisoner to answer him. His silence weighed down upon him. He saw that the Prisoner had listened carefully all the time, looking gently in his face. But evidently he did not want to reply. The old man longed for Him to say something, however bitter and terrible. But He suddenly approached the old man in silence and softly kissed him on the forehead. That was his answer. The old man shuddered. His lips moved. He went to the door, opened it and said to him: 'Go, and come no more. . . . Come not at all, never, never!' And he led Him out into the dark alleys of the town. The Prisoner went away".
> "And the old man?" [This is Alyosha's question.]
> "The kiss glows in his heart, but the old man adheres to his idea."
> "And you with him, you too?" cried Alyosha mournfully.

There is of course no exact parallel between this story and the passion narrative. It is as if Dostoevsky's intent was to encapsulate Christ's silence before Pilate and his words of forgiveness on the cross into a single scene where a kiss conveys the heart of Christ's redemptive power. The kiss of Christ, which "glows" in the old man's heart, is certainly not a kiss of approval, nor is it simply a kiss of understanding. It could be categorized as a kiss of forgiveness or acceptance despite the unacceptableness of the cardinal's actions. The difficulty with even that categorization is its incompleteness: it does not describe the feeling communicated in the kiss. I want to argue that what the old man felt can best be described as Christ's suffering love for him.

The history of the cardinal's life, his understanding of human possibilities, his uses of authority and power stand in opposition to the life and teaching of Christ. But Christ does not allow this opposition to break his relation to the cardinal. This is true despite the fact that the specific form of the cardinal's opposition is betrayal of Christ and the community which seeks to embody the spirit of Christ. The kiss of Christ, which continues to glow in the old man's heart, says, "though you have broken your relation to me, I will not break my relation to you."

In the novel, Dostoevsky parallels the relation between Christ and the Grand Inquisitor with that between Alyosha and Ivan. Alyosha is devastated not by the story, but by the fact that Ivan, his beloved brother, conceived it. He sees it as a story that only a bitter person, longing for death could compose. Under Alyosha's troubled questions, Ivan confesses that he is able to endure life only by living as if "everything is lawful." Alyosha is stunned by this reply and falls silent. Finally, Ivan says,

> "I thought that in going away from here I have you at least . . . but now I see that there is no place for me even in your heart, my dear hermit. The formula, 'all is lawful,' I won't renounce. Will you renounce me for that, yes?"
> Alyosha got up, went to him and softly kissed him on the lips.
> "That's plagiarism," cried Ivan, highly delighted. "You stole that from my poem [story]. Thank you though."

Alyosha "steals" from the story: he allows the pattern of Christ to become his pattern. He identifies with Christ or, better still, he finds his identity in Christ, so that Christ's power can be expressed through his actions. But what is the nature of that power?

It is certainly not controlling power. The kiss swerves neither the cardinal nor Ivan from their original intent. Yet the kiss moves them; also, they are grateful for it. Something unexpectedly powerful has happened to them or has been communicated to them.

Some years ago Daniel Day Williams, an American theologian, commented upon the fact that the reception of one person's feeling by another without rejection constitutes a basic factor in psychological therapy. He went on to write:

> The communication of feeling to the other in the accepting situation constitutes a new standpoint in which the self may reorder and reinterpret its experience. . . . When the feelings are received in "love" there is a transmutation which takes on the quality of the love which is given. (Daniel Day Williams, "How Does God Act" in W. L. Reese and E. Freeman, eds., *Process and Divinity* [LaSalle, IL: Open Court Publishing Co., 1964] pp. 176–77.)

The two interchanges before us—that between Christ and the Inquisitor and Alyosha and Ivan—suggest Williams' "accepting situation." Acceptance does not necessarily mean approval. Perhaps we find some help here in the Gospel story of the woman caught in adultery (John 8:1–11). Jesus' refusal to condemn the woman does not mean that he approves of adulterous relations. But he does accept the woman in a way her accusers do not. Similarly the cardinal's betrayal and Ivan's attitude are not being approved. What is being accepted is what it feels like to be the cardinal and Ivan. This feeling, the feeling of the other, without rejection, communicates itself as love to that other. Love, of course, cannot be coercive; it respects rather than overrides the freedom of the other. Also, its powers of renewal and transformation depend, in part, upon being received in love. If the adulterous woman merely feels Christ as using her misfortune to put down his enemies, then she disables the redemptive power in Christ's forgiving action. Christ's action creates a new standpoint for the woman, but if she does not receive Christ in love, she will not perceive the new point on which to stand. The Gospel does not tell us how the woman responded to Christ. But Dostoevsky's story suggests that the cardinal and Ivan receive in love the Christlike action upon them. They, at least, can see for themselves another standpoint, another way (God's way?) to order their selves and their relations to others.

In the therapeutic situation, we are at times a little inattentive to the painful cost of acceptance, perhaps because the therapist can temporarily bracket or lay aside the question of approval. But Christ who goes to the cross cannot bracket that question. He has been betrayed by the other, and he feels that betrayal quite directly. The direct experience of betrayal is felt as pain. Dostoevsky's Inquisitor knows he has caused Christ pain. He waits for, even wants, Christ "to say something, however bitter and terrible." Similarly Ivan knows that his despairing, cynical attitude to life must cause suffering to Alyosha. He expects that suffering to lead Alyosha to renounce him. That is, both the Grand Inquisitor and Ivan expect the pain that they cause another to issue into the other's wrath-like condemnation. Instead they receive loving acceptance. But if the pain does not get expressed in the wrath, what has happened to it?

We are back to the discovery that God's love for us, if it is not to be defeated and turned into wrath, must become suffering love. God's love of the betrayer is only possible by taking the pain within, rather than directing it wrath-like upon the other. The pain is not being repressed. Quite the contrary. It becomes that new ingredient in the relationship that allows the relationship to be maintained despite the fact that one of the members continually breaks it. Christ's love for a cardinal who betrays him and the church must either turn into destructive wrath and break the relationship, or into suffering love which maintains the relation despite continued betrayal.

The literary Christ in *The Brothers Karamazov* draws its power from being an analogue to the Christ of the Gospels and to the Christ we know in our faith. It is a source of insight for us precisely to the extent that it stays true to and throws light upon our own experience of Christ's healing, renewing, reconciling, transformative work. But can Dostoevsky's christological narrative help us with the vexing question of the causal element in Christ's suffering love?

Alyosha's and Christ's suffering love prevents neither Ivan nor the cardinal from pursuing their destructive paths. Love's willingness to endure pain—as the price of staying in a relation to the other—does not exert coercive or controlling power on the other. This seems to be true to our experience, both personal and political. Also, Christ does not promise nor does his life ever suggest that love of our enemies guarantees their transformation into our brothers and sisters in Christ. But this does not mean that love is not causal. We are much too inclined to identify causal power as coercive power. But not all causal powers are coercive. We can see this by considering the ways parents' actions and values affect the lives of their children. Of course some parents' actions are controlling—such as the parental decision to live in this house, in this city, rather than in some other house, in some other city. But the great bulk of parents' actions upon their children leave them with a measure of freedom to respond. Certainly, some parents seek to control their children. But children tend to resist, one way or another, parental control. Despite this, we think of parents as a causal, sometimes the most significant causal, element in a person's life.

The love that Dostoevsky's Christ bears to the cardinal is not controlling. The cardinal's integrity of person, his freedom of response, is left intact. The earlier quote from Williams suggests that the causal element in Christ's love—in this case for the Cardinal—lies in constituting "a new standpoint in which the self may re-order and reinterpret its experience." This is a non-coercive, non-controlling form of causality. Is it a redemptive form of causality?

We can answer this question by imagining an alternate sequence of events. Let us suppose that the Christ in the story responds to the cardinal with wrathful words. The cardinal expects to be condemned—he has, after all, gone so far as to accuse Christ of hindering the necessary work of the church—so that Christ's condemnation of him, no matter how terrible, would not alter the situation. The cardinal's standpoint or assessment of what is possible and what is not possible would remain unchanged. Indeed, it would simply be continued. He believes that he and not Christ has a more realistic view of human needs and human possibilities. The cardinal is that familiar figure of authority who holds himself in such high esteem that he cannot see that he is neither as good nor as right as he thinks he is.

Dostoevsky writes the scene this way, because when he thinks of the cardinal he is looking beyond judgment to the possibility of transformation and redemption. He can think this way partly because he knows that ultimately God's forgiving love is a little oblivious to morals. That affects the way he understands Christ's mode of power. Into the apparently impenetrable situation of a powerful official's righteous certainty, Dostoevsky portrays a Christ who comes not with denunciatory power but with a kiss—a kiss which communicates a love which has internalized the pain of betrayal. The cardinal experiences not the expected condemnation of Christ, but a love that refuses to let go, no matter what. In this story, Christ is released and not burned as originally planned. Dostoevsky seems to be suggesting that Christ's love can penetrate even where penetration appears impossible.

Still, there is no suggestion that the cardinal changes his policies. Does this mean that Christ lacks potency? Would Christ be more potent if Dostoevsky had a host of angels appear with flaming swords to impress upon the cardinal the need to change his actions and self-understanding? Would Christ be more potent if instead of dying on the cross, a host of angels had appeared to help him down?

Perhaps the phrase "more potent" merely sows confusion. There is, obviously, potency in coercive power. The state has that kind of power in relation to its citizens; and it delegates that power to its officials. The cardinal has coercive power over Christ (as did Pilate before him) because he has the arm of the state behind him. It is not that Christ has less of that kind of power, but that he cannot have that kind of power at all and still be Christ. The reason is that coercive power ignores, even threatens, the integrity of the other's self. When the cardinal, in his work as Grand Inquisitor, uses the power of the state to compel confessions of faith, he is not redeeming lost souls, but threatening whatever integrity of self a person may have. People who confess what they do not believe, even if those confessions are made under torture, may lose that modicum of self-respect which makes their lives worth-while. The only kind of power which can redeem is one which allows for transformation without violating the integrity and freedom of the self.

Walker Percy has raised for us the dismal question whether, in the end, the world yields only to violence. If that were the case, then it is not redemption we are looking toward, but annihilation of the opposing other. But if the opposing other, our hateful enemy, is also the beloved of God, how is annihilation a victory? And if we, in our own small ways, are betrayers of God, how is a final annihilation a victory?

Let us look at a story told by the exiled Russian poet Joseph Brodsky, in a commencement address published in the *New York Review of Books* (16 August 1984):

Twenty years ago the following scene took place in one of the numerous prison yards of northern Russia: At 7:00 A.M. the door of a cell was flung open and on its threshold stood a prison guard who addressed its inmates: "Citizens! the collective of this prison's guards challenges you, the inmates, to socialist competition in cutting the lumber amassed in our yard." In those parts there is no central heating, and the local police, in a manner of speaking, tax all the nearby lumber companies for one-tenth of their produce. By the time I am describing, the prison yard looked like a veritable lumberyard. The piles were two to three stories high, dwarfing the one-storied quadrangle of the prison itself. The need for cutting was evident, although socialist competition of this sort had happened before. "And what if I refuse to take part in this?" inquired one of the inmates. "Well, in that case, no meals for you," replied the guard. Then axes were issued to inmates, and the cutting started. Both prisoners and guards worked in earnest, and by noon, all of them, especially the always underfed prisoners, were exhausted. A break was announced and people sat down to eat—except the fellow who asked the question. He kept swinging his axe. Both prisoners and guards exchanged jokes about him, something about Jews being normally regarded as smart people whereas this man . . . and so forth. After the break they resumed the work, although in a somewhat more flagging manner. By 4:00 P.M. the guards quit, since for them it was the end of their shift; a bit later the inmates stopped too. The man's axe kept swinging. Several times he was urged to stop, by both parties, but he paid no attention. It seemed as though he had acquired a certain rhythm he was unwilling to break; or was it a rhythm that possessed him? To the others, he looked like an automaton. By 5:00, by 6:00, the axe was still going up and down. Both guards and inmates were now watching him keenly, and the sardonic expressions on their faces gradually gave way first to one of bewilderment and then to one of terror. By 7:30 the man stopped, staggered into his cell, and fell asleep. For the rest of his stay in that prison, no call for socialist competition between guards and inmates was issued again. Although the wood kept piling up.

Brodsky's intent in telling this story is to suggest a mode of resistance, a strategy, for some dark hour in which we confront overwhelmingly powerful forces of evil. He wants us to remember, as the prisoner remembered, that Christ's advice on cheek-turning was followed by the injunction to give to those who demand your coat your cloak as well, and to walk two miles with those who compel you to go one. This teaching must not be understood as *passive* resistance, Brodsky warns; it is active resistance for a victim stripped of all resources except that of his spirit and his arms and legs.

Brodsky's story yields more than strategy; it can help us in our own search for the causal element in suffering love. It focuses on a particular aspect in the act of suffering that disables evil by rendering it absurd or meaningless in the eyes of the oppressor.

The inmate's overworked axe, like Christ's kiss to the Grand Inquisitor, seeks other means to defeat evil than by inflicting violence or moral condemnation on an oppressor—in this case the guards or prison authorities. That axe, by its excess of compliance with the guards' commands, alters the perspective of the guards so that they find themselves reinterpreting the meaning of their command. The prisoner's response to a command, which had seemed vested with power and purpose, has so divested it of its original meaning as to communicate to the guards a sense of their own helpless absurdity.

The guards can deal with physical rebellion; they are trained for that. Perhaps, like the Grand Inquisitor, the guards may expect, even want, the prisoners to condemn them morally, no doubt because they are prepared for it. Evildoers are quite capable of immunizing themselves to cries of moral outrage. The conscience of the unjust, even when momentarily aroused, is easily quelled. What the unjust, or anyone else, cannot quell is the loss of vitality that comes in the wake of a sense of meaninglessness. When our lives lose meaning, our spirits are drained of the very power by which we affirm ourselves. The loss of meaning is the spirit's sickness unto death.

We tend to think of meaninglessness as an inherent evil, and of meaning as an inherent good. When we do so we are a little hasty in our judgment. We forget that some of the things that inject meaning into our lives work to the destruction of others. Thousands of Germans suffering inwardly from their nation's defeat in the first World War found meaning and new life in the Nazi movement. But that kind of meaning led to a re-militarized Germany and another World War. Similarly, racist and anti-Semitic attitudes and actions offer meaning to people by providing them with a sense of identity which otherwise they might have been lacking. When people whom we might not otherwise notice—and who may be hardly noticeable to themselves—say, "I am an anti-Semite," "I am a member of the Klan," "I am a Nazi," etc., they gain our attention and, in a morbid way, even our interest. In all these instances, the healing or redemption of such people would involve their experiencing the meaninglessness of their perspective. Brodsky's story suggests that certain kinds of suffering can contribute to the redemptive process by communicating to evildoers the absurdity or meaninglessness of their perspective. We need to look at Jesus' life in the light of this insight.

Much has been made recently of Jesus' defying cultural and religious customs in engaging women in public and theological debate (e. g., the story of the Syro-Phoenician woman), or even in encouraging women toward discipleship (e. g., the story of Mary and Martha). In breaking Jewish custom, Jesus risked ridicule. To most of his fellow Jews he would appear a ludicrous figure standing in a public place debating a woman on points of theology. That is one side of the story. It finds its parallel in the Brodsky tale at that point where the guards and prisoners find contemptuous the inmate's failure to take a lunch break. The other side of the story is that Jesus' sustained treatment of women with the kind of respect that his culture restricted to men renders ridiculous the sex role traditions of his society. Or more accurately, for those who call Jesus Lord, his authority empties meaning out of a particular social custom. But Jesus cannot do this without suffering—in this case, by drawing social ridicule upon himself. In other words, Jesus pays a price to overcome the evil of a social custom which relegates women to secondary status. We must be careful not to make light of that price, as if Jesus were immune from the social and inner pain consequent upon defying a deeply entrenched cultural norm.

The point is not that Jesus was a feminist. That says a little too much and much too little about him. Rather, there is a pattern in his life of defying those social customs which degrade people and hinder the power of God's creative love in a person's life. It was said of Jesus that he received sinners and ate with them. Whatever we think of this now, it is clear enough that *then* it counted against him in the eyes of socially established people. Jesus was willing to heal on the Sabbath, though by so doing he outraged religious people. He gave his sympathy and power to the poor, sick, and outcast, rather than to those who considered themselves the righteous remnant of Israel. The Gospels suggest throughout that the righteous and the established authorities let Jesus know that they were offended by the way he expressed his concern for the welfare of powerless people.

Jesus is remembered as living for others in a way that seemed heedless of the consequences to himself. But "living for others" does not yet catch that factor which could trigger the hostility that would bring him to the cross. Jesus lived for others in a way that brought upon him social disapproval and ridicule. The painful consequences of his actions were as important to the expression of his ministry as the actions themselves. The authenticity of his concern for others was communicated not simply by his willingness to bear negative consequences, but by his actions evoking these consequences. His suffering for others and on account of others is what makes his life into empowered love. Without that suffering Jesus would have been received as no more than another idealistic dreamer for whom the verbal expression of conviction was sufficient for a life's work. In fact, of course, the opposite was the case. Jesus' refusal at Gethsemane to step off the path that would now clearly take him to the cross was consistent with the whole course of his ministry, which communicated love to the other through his willingness to suffer for the other.

This communication of love helps us make sense of the irony that Jesus cannot stand against the evil of suffering without suffering the evil of the cross. Of course, the cross in itself does not communicate love. It was the way in which the Roman Empire communicated the painful price of running afoul of the state and the established authorities.

The great fact of Christian faith is that the suffering of Jesus on the cross communicates more than his pain. We feel renewing, creative powers in his suffering. Part of the reason for this is that Jesus took on suffering as the speech of love so that he quite literally suffered for the sake of communication to others. There is a voluntary, creative element in his suffering so that it might be helpful to think of this as active suffering in distinction from passive suffering. For example, the suffering of the robbers who hung alongside Jesus is passive suffering. Or, to go farther afield, a child suffering from a broken arm or a humiliation in school or a congenitally weak heart is suffering passively. The parent, suffering from the child's suffering and communicating love to the child through that suffering, is manifesting suffering in its active form. The child feels as healing, in some small way and perhaps sometimes in a large way, the suffering love of the parent. Imagine what would be communicated to the child if his or her pain was met by the cool indifference of the parent.

This distinction between active and passive suffering takes us a little further along in our analysis of the Brodsky story. The prisoner suffers physically from chopping wood all day. Perhaps he suffers inwardly from having been humiliated by the guard. Had he merely complied with the order of the guards, he would have been a victim passively suffering his fate. By complying excessively he increased his physical suffering, but he also turned the tables on the guards. Now they were suffering inwardly. Their power as agents of evil had turned from a feeling of enhancement to a feeling of absurdity. The prisoner had been able to do this by finding a way to turn passive suffering into active suffering. In this way he not only says "No" to the evil of inflicting suffering on others but he undermines the sense of meaning that supports those who serve the forces of evil.

Still, this story will not yield us insight into the power of Christ's suffering if it takes us no further than to suggest a table-turning strategy for a seemingly helpless victim of agents of evil. We are left uneasy with the question whether the prisoner's suffering can be understood as a suffering for another and as a communication of love. Does Brodsky's story constitute anything more that a bit of practical advice for an individual in a tough scrape?

We can see beyond the individualistic dimension in this story by noting that the strategy employed by the prisoner is non-violent: it works by disabling the power of evil in the heart and mind of the oppressor. For this reason, it reminds us of the social strategies developed by Gandhi in the Indian independence movement and by Martin Luther King, Jr., in the American civil rights movement. In these movements, the intent of the strategy is to effect both social change and the inner transformation of the oppressor. Brodsky's use of a christological teaching—the excess of compliance—throws light on why non-violence is effective in a social movement. But the relevance of this teaching to a social movement suggests how it can be understood as a suffering for others and a communication of love.

Civil rights demonstrators who continue to march peaceably, or who quietly maintain a sit-in, though water hoses may be trained on them or dogs stand ready to be set on them or electric rods are poised to prod them are complying—though excessively so—with the state's desires that its citizens behave decently and orderly in public places. By not resisting the violence of the police, by taking as little note of that violence as possible, by going limp when apprehended, they make police violence appear absurd—certainly to those who watch the scene on national television news, but also to the very police who are the agents of the violence. The police, like Brodsky's guards, experience the tables turned on them. The outer suffering they are inflicting on others is not reinforcing them in their role as agents of violence. Instead, it is leading them to the kind of inner suffering which can become an occasion to transform their conscience. In this way, the civil rights demonstrators, and Brodsky's prisoner, can be understood as suffering for others. Their suffering leads the police and the onlooker toward a new standpoint. It is possible for the police to begin, even if only in a small way, to question their service to forces of evil. But they are being led in a non-coercive way. Their integrity and freedom remain respected. Thus, the strategy of excessive compliance is a communication of love in the same way as Christ's kiss to the Grand Inquisitor was a communication of suffering love.

When the police beat the oppressed, it appears that once again, violence has had the last word. But when the defeat of the beaten one communicates to the victor not meaning but absurdity, then both violence and defeat require a new interpretation. Violence becomes a crisis to itself and defeat appears with power. This pattern, which emerges from the analysis of a non-violent, non-coercive social movement is, of course, the pattern of Christ on the cross. It is the pattern of God's christological power—so utterly different from our assumptions and expectations, and even, perhaps, from our hopes. The cross, as revelation, helps us to redefine our understanding of redemptive power. As we stand under it, it also comes to reshape our hopes, so that what we live toward moves into closer approximation to God's good will for us.

In first-century Palestine, the great majority of Jews interpreted the cross as a sure sign of Jesus' failure to establish himself as the expected Christ. It was not the lack of passionate desire that made Jews reject Jesus. They longed for the Christ because he was a sign of the coming kingdom, the kingdom that would vindicate God's righteousness and erase all evil, injustice, and pain. The cross stood as a shocking reversal of their expectation.

Jesus, of course, was a first-century Jew. We have every reason to believe that he shared in the hopes and understanding of his own people. His remembered words of forsakenness on the cross are so startling as to suggest that he too experienced the cross as failure. This may strike us as an odd and even blasphemous thing to say. But we need to note the difference between the experience of failure and being ruled by failure. Jesus saw the cross increasingly looming before him. Yet his strong sense that he was on God's path kept him from swerving, despite the disaster ahead. At Gethsemane, Jesus prays that "this cup" be taken from him—unless it be God's will that he take it. That he "took it" means two things: he had come to terms with the fact that his life—according to his and his people's expectation—would end in failure; and second, he counted it more important to maintain communion with God than to take measures which would avoid failure. Had he taken those measures, he might have been able to save his life, but then he would not have been the Christ. That he could refuse to save himself from the cross, despite the pressure of his religious assumptions and his own psychological anxiety, lies in the mystery of his communion with God. One way of stating the form of this

communion is by thinking in terms of an identity or fusion of wills.
Jesus had so identified his will with God's will that he was able to
sacrifice his hopes to God's actions in and through him. With this
perspective in mind, we can say that at the cross Jesus presents his
failed life to God. But then we go on to say that we experience Jesus
as Lord and Christ because we find God in this life acting
definitively to heal and transform the human community. But when
we say this we have committed ourselves to a reunderstanding of
failure—and success.

The failure that Jesus presents to God is his defeat at the
hands of the violent and the powerful. Jesus had lived his life so as to
give strength to the weak: the sick, the poor, the possessed, the
handicapped, the sinner, the outsider. His way of caring for the
many evoked the opposition of the mighty and the self-righteous.
They had the power to put him to death. The fact that they had this
power raises a crisis for faith. It is not simply a crisis of temporarily
dashed hopes for the coming kingdom. It is a crisis brought about by
a world where, ever anon, victory is achieved through violence, and
triumph belongs to the strong. Those who care for the weak seem
themselves to be weak, for they are trodden down by history, and
appear to be abandoned even by God.

The crisis that comes to faith expresses itself at first in the
question, "Why, God?" but when we have cried our hearts out,
another question comes to us, "Why care?" Why care about the
weak in a world where the violence of the powerful controls and
destroys human lives and human relationships?

The resurrection of Christ is sometimes invoked as the
Christian answer to evil. The thought is that the resurrection of
Christ heralds our own resurrection, and that the raising of the
faithful from death to eternal life provides, in itself, sufficient
justification for the few, short years of earthly suffering from pain,
injustice, and death. Sadly, there are difficulties in this response
that are not unlike those found in the apocalyptic answer. It forces
us to weigh unbearable horror now against unspeakable joy later.
But how does a later joy justify an earlier horror? And it leaves evil
on earth largely untouched. It neither transforms nor redeems evil;
it simply moves life to a plane where evil has no sway.

Still, Christian faith is resurrection faith so that we are right to look at the resurrection of Christ in our struggle with the problem and power of evil.

The Apostles' experience of the resurrected Christ as Lord—however vaguely we may have to leave the definition of that experience—does tell us that the Jesus who in his earthly life identified himself with God's love has shown in his resurrected life that God has identified with him. The resurrection of Christ means that God says "Yes" to the life of Jesus: "Yes" to a life that cares for others, suffers with the injustices to others, forgives the sins committed by others. The resurrection says "Yes" to Jesus. Is the spirit in this life God's Spirit? Yes. Is the suffering in this life God's suffering? Yes. Is the power in this life, God's power? Yes.

Jesus on the cross presents his failure to God. It is the failure of suffering love to coerce a loving response. But this defeat on the cross redefines failure for the Christian—and for the church. In his defeat, Christ denies the identification of God's power with coercion. Now it is a sign of failure to resort to coercive powers. In his defeat at the hands of the strong, Christ makes it a victory to identify with and care for the weak. Now it is a sign of failure to live with indifference to the suffering of the weak.

At the cross, Jesus presents to God a life that enables God to do a new thing. Through that life, God draws forth a new people formed and informed by the spirit of Jesus Christ. Now there is a new community which by definition comes into itself by standing against structures and actions of evil and injustice, and by providing loving support to those who have suffered evil in any of its myriad forms, and by forgiving, always forgiving, those who need forgiveness.

We began chapters ago with the question "Why, God?" And now we have come upon the question "Why care?" But the answer to the question "Why care?" is not simply the universal one that "God cares." The answer is that God's caring has brought into being a particular, living body of caring whose head is Christ. I am speaking, of course, of the church, to whom I have a few words to address.

A Letter to the Church:
Placing the Answer

We must never tire of remembering who we are and what our purpose is. We are a living body of caring, issuing from and expressing Christ's continuing, redemptive power. As such, we are the answer to those questions of suffering and evil that rise out of our lives and onto our lips. But we are a living answer, not a dogmatic answer. Our primary response to evil is not one of explanation but of witness. We point to a place where the evil from which we suffer can be engaged, and its destructive power diminished, and even dissipated.

The claim of Christian faith is that in a particular place, in the life of a community of sisters and brothers in Christ, there is a way—a way of worship, a way of being open toward others and God, a way of listening, a way of seeing, a way of acting—which can counter the power of evil in all our lives, and set us on our feet again. This is not a claim of exclusivity, as if here alone God's power over evil is present. It is a claim of universality, or better still, it is an invitation to universality: all are invited to participate here in God's great healing powers.

Come back with me now to the spring of 1965, to the time just after my daughter's death, to that afternoon's theological talk with my friend, the ordained minister and graduate student. His answer to my anguished cry for help in understanding had been, "We are waiting for you to help us." At the time, that response felt empty of meaning, even unfair. It seemed to evade my question and it placed the responsibility for the answer on me. Yet that conversation marked a turning point. When I gained some distance, I saw it not as avoiding the answer but as suggesting the place where the answer begins.

My friend did not take the path of a Joban comforter. He did not tell me that evil was a mystery which lay within God's providential purposes or even that I must not expect answers to far-reaching questions. His refusal to "comfort" me this way was not a matter of tact, as if this were an inappropriate time to suggest that God has good and loving reasons to will or permit the woes that afflict us. If anything, his tone of voice, his walk, the expression on his face, told me that he did not believe for a minute that God either caused this death or had the power to prevent it. Also, his words, "We are waiting for you to help us," did not say that there was no theological answer. Quite the reverse was implied. His words held out the hope that there was an answer, but that the answer must come from the believer who endured the suffering. More significantly, there is a "we" who waits with the suffering believer for whom the answer is a matter of life and death, faith and unfaith.

What does this "waiting with" consist of? First of all, caring presence. My friend was waiting with me on that afternoon walk, as were those who sat with us during those terrible days immediately following the death of our child, as were those who would write us, even years later, on the day of Jennifer's death, or Samuel's death. Their presence expressed their compassion. They offered suffering companionship as their way of helping us live through the death of a child.

Hope and listening were also part of their "waiting with." The hope was that their compassion and tears would make present for us God's compassion and tears, and that we would gain strength from the divine presence. Later I realized that they were listening, and continued to listen, for some sign of God's comforting presence in our lives.

For my part, I hardly knew what I was waiting for. I called upon God the comforter, but God did not come. I cried out to the void, and heard only the silence. Still, I went on with my life—my work, my family, my worship, my politics. And above the pained and ever-whispered "No," I began to hear some new sounds: my own laughter, my own singing, my own sounds of joy. I listened to myself, and heard the power of God's "Yes" prevailing amid my sorrow and pain, and I knew that God the comforter had never left me. Those who had waited with me had not waited or hoped in vain. Where they had gathered, God was present in the power of suffering love.

I do not intend to sentimentalize the church. Those of us involved in the life of the church know only too well how divisive, unsympathetic, and narrow-minded we are capable of being. Christ is present where we gather, but Christ is not the only power present to us. Those other powers that draw us, and whose values we pursue, are legion. We know them by the name of nation, people, class, race, ethnic group, religious denomination, fellowship society, family, and so on. We belong to these groups. They give us our identity and we give them our loyalty. Rightly so. We need to be loyal to the sources of our identity; there is much good in them and in their histories. But these histories are also riddled with violence, hostility, exploitation, and humiliation. Lodged in the collective mind of each of us—American and Russian, Israeli and Arab, Afrikaner and African, Irish Protestant and Irish Catholic, Jew and Christian, Black and White, male and female—is a memory of destruction, a past filled with enemies and adversaries. Our "identity crisis" is not that we cannot find an identity, but that the identity we find inherits a history of destructive powers.

The finding of our identity always occurs within the life and history of a people. Those of us who enter into the life of the church come with our separate histories, our identity according to sex, class, race, nation, family, etc. We do not cease to be "Jew or Greek," "male or female," so to speak. But this renewing community offers a new place to locate our identity: in Jesus Christ. In Christ, we take our identify from one who is brother and sister to all, and who calls each of us into his history of healing, reconciling and transforming. Perhaps it would be more accurate to say that we live into our identity by our continual participation in Christ's redemptive power.

Paul says, "For as many of you as were baptized into Christ have put on Christ" (Gal. 3:27). The church in which we are baptized is one body with many members. All people are invited into membership. The invitation is irrevocable. In this community our old enemies from our old histories are seen as our potential sisters and brothers; here, the stranger to whose plight we were indifferent becomes the one in whom we find Christ. When we "put on Christ," we place ourselves in a community and on a path which has no end but God's kingdom, a kingdom of continually transforming love. To this end, we witness by word and act. In living out this witness, we live in God's redemptive powers; in witnessing with this living, we give to others, and to ourselves, Christian faith's answer to evil.